GREAT COLLEGES FOR THE REAL WORLD

Get In. Get. Out. Get a Job.

378.025 VIO

THIRD EDITION
MICHAEL VIOLLT

OCTAMERON
ASSOCIATES

© Copyright 2002 by Michael P. Viollt
All rights reserved

No part of this book may be reproduced in any form, by photostat, microfilm, xerography, or any other means, or incorporated into any information retrieval system, electronic or mechanical, without written permission of the copyright owner. Violations of this provision will be vigorously prosecuted.

Care and diligence have been taken in preparing the data contained herein, however, Octameron does not guarantee its accuracy.

Address editorial correspondence to:

Octameron Associates
PO Box 2748
Alexandria, VA 22301
703/836-5480 (voice)
703/836-5650 (fax)

info@octameron.com (e-mail)
www.octameron.com

ISBN 1-57509-084-8

PRINTED IN THE UNITED STATES OF AMERICA

CONTENTS

A New Model 4

College Choices in the Past 5

The Changing World 6
Government Regulations • Types of Financial Aid • The Cost of Education • The Changing Job Market • Economic Realities • Technology • Entrepreneurial Climate • Lack of Common Morality • View of Shared Heritage

The New Selection Process 8
Undergraduate Enrollment • Proximity to a Major City • Admission Standards • College Costs • Average Financial Aid Award • Retention to Graduation • Student Diversity • Placement Services • Enrollment Growth • Program Strengths • Control Status • Average Class Size • Majors Available • General Education • Early Skills Development • Advisory System

Selecting a College Major 11
Six Clusters of Majors • Where the Jobs Are

Evaluating Personal Needs 14
Learning Style • Personality Type • Aptitudes, Strengths and Weaknesses • College Expectations • Personal Commitment

What Makes a College Ideal for You? 16

Secret Indicators for Selecting a College 18
Growth • Emphasis • Facilities • Scholarships • Majors • Student Needs • Materials • Campus Visits

How the "Best 201" Were Selected 20

How to Use the College Profile Sheets 21

Endnotes 22

Quiz: Are the Colleges in This Book Right for You? 23

The "Best 201" Colleges 24

A New Model

Students attend college for many different reasons. A college education can offer a sense of purpose, an opportunity for growth, a chance to develop a philosophy of life, a time to gain an appreciation of the arts, a chance to explore interests, and a window to one's weaknesses. Historically, it has also been about finding oneself, gaining confidence, and developing social skills; however, for the majority of today's students, it is mostly about career preparation and advancement.

Students have to weigh both career and non-career considerations in their college choice. When doing this, it is important to remember that college is a huge investment of time and money, and most of us expect to see real return on any investment we make—especially when it is one of the biggest we will make in our lives. A college education can easily cost more than $120,000 in real expenses and at least that much, again, in income lost while still in school. Yet, in spite of this cost, the number of Americans attending college is increasing every year. In the past, over 60 percent of high school graduates were going on to college; projections indicate that by 2005 that number will increase to 75 percent.

Going to college is no longer a luxury. In today's labor market, competition for choice positions can be fierce and almost all good positions require at least some post-secondary training. A college degree is becoming a requirement for more and more occupations and offers a huge lifetime earnings advantage. The average HS graduate earned $24,110 in 1998 compared to $44,740 for the average bachelor's degree holder.[1] Over a working lifetime, the college graduate can expect to earn three times what a HS graduate will make. This earnings differential is why finding a college where you can be successful is not only important but a financial necessity.

Today's college students fall into two main groups:
- The first group is made up of working adults trying to upgrade their skills to advance in their career or to start a new one. For most of these students, college is a vehicle to job or career growth.
- The second group, often referred to as "traditional students" are recent high school graduates who are beginning to explore and build their first-professional careers. Most in this group are looking at college as a career builder.

When you combine these groups, it is easy to see why the majority of students report that career and job development are their primary motivation for attending college.[2] Yet many colleges are slow in responding to this change in demand for education that is career-focused and applied-skill based. This student demand is a radical change from 30 years ago, and many colleges are still using the old model.

Many undergraduate colleges and universities are too steeped in tradition, managed by committees, focused on research, and staffed by teaching assistants to adapt to a changing world. They are heavily invested in buildings, and often located in remote locations far away from large population centers. They are often resistant to change.[3] As strange as it seems, meeting consumer demand is foreign to some colleges. The colleges presented in this book have changed in an attempt to deliver what students want. These are colleges that are within your reach, with programs to match your needs, and that can be completed in a reasonable time frame. They feature programs that offer a tangible return on your investment in the form of a job or career path.

If you put career development at the top of your list of college expectations and did not graduate at the head of your high school class, then you are in the majority, and will probably be interested in the colleges presented in this book. These colleges may not be featured in magazine articles about the best colleges, but they may be the right choice for you and your busy lifestyle. Some may not be the obvious first choice; however, in many cases they should be. They are colleges that take to heart the needs of the student as a consumer and are a great fit for the student with above-average ambition. Take a minute to complete the short survey in the appendix to see if these colleges are a good fit for you.

College Choices in the Past

During the last decade, the profile of the "typical" college student has changed dramatically. Today, only about 15 percent of all college students will be recent high school graduates who pack their bags and go away to college.[4] Today's student is more likely to be a financially-independent working adult balancing college with family, social activities, work, and other responsibilities. They are a different type of student with different goals than past generations which has led to a need to rethink the criteria used for selecting a college.

Unfortunately, many of the books available to help students make their college choices still use selection criteria relevant for the 1930s, 1940s, and 1950s. In the past, when selecting a college, students would often look at a list of criteria similar to the one that follows:

- Academic Reputation of the College
- Social Organizations Active on the Campus
- Athletic Programs Available
- Distance from Home to College
- Gender Make-up of Students
- Religious Affiliation of the College
- Research Orientation of the Faculty
- Size of the Total Campus
- Kinds of Housing Available
- Student Mix
- Campus Setting

While some of these criteria are still important, they miss critical issues like total college cost and career development opportunities. They also tend to view the selection process from perspectives that no longer apply. This book's goal is to help you develop new selection criteria that let you max-imize the return on your college education investment of time and money.

The Changing World

Higher education continues to become more and more focused on applied-career skills and credential development.[5] Most of today's students report that career development is a primary reason for attending college. They agree that general education is important; however, they want general education that develops career supportive skills, is structured rather than haphazard, and develops lifelong learning foundations. This is all in response to a changing world. Dramatic social changes have fueled this resurgence of interest in career and vocationalism. The pace of this evolution has accelerated tremendously in the last few years. Many reasons are given for this change, but several stand out.

Government Regulations

Changes in the financial aid laws are designed to make colleges more accountable, outlining clearly defined expectations. Government at both the state and federal level is demanding more in the way of results from the government dollars invested in higher education. This has forced colleges to find ways to add measurable value to education through enhanced services, including such things as improved job placement for graduates.

Types of Financial Aid

At the same time, scholarships and grants from government sources have declined as a percent of tuition and have been replaced with a variety of student loans. In other words, today's students have fewer grant dollars and more loan debt as a percent of tuition—their out-of-pocket costs have increased and they now have much more at stake.[6] Because of this, they expect to see a tangible return in the way of a good job or career advancement at graduation.

The Cost of Education—A Huge Investment

The cost of education has increased dramatically, outpacing inflation over the last 25 years. This has resulted in the total cost of today's college education becoming a larger share of a family's annual income than it was in the past. For the neediest families, it has gone from 42 percent of household income in 1977 to 61 percent today.[7] This problem is compounded when you consider that the number of years students now take to earn a bachelor's degree has increased from four to well over five. In fact, fewer than 30 percent of students now finish college in four years. This results in extra years of college expense and, more importantly, additional years of opportunity costs in the form of lost wages and experience. The time you spend in school is lost working time as well as lost career-advancement time. A good college choice can decrease this total cost.

The Changing Job Market

Large companies no longer do the largest share of hiring. Most new jobs are in companies with 100 or fewer employees. In these smaller firms, there is no room for expensive formal training programs. Individuals are expected to hit the ground running. They need a usable skill beginning on day one. This is especially true in the information technology sector, where over 70 percent of job creation is in small firms.[8]

Even in large corporations, formal training designed to make new college graduates productive is no longer the norm. As companies compete in a global market, the drive toward efficient operations has forced every employee to be a productive member of the team. Middle management, once the realm of college graduates, has been "reengineered." Teams of employees often share responsibility. These teams look for a contribution from every member.

The skills required by employers in an information age are very different from those developed by "departmentalized" college majors that are centered on traditional learning objectives with research orientations. Today's graduates must learn how to compete by developing information-management skills no matter what their field of study. They need a broad set of skills that can be applied in a variety of functional areas that are in a constant state of change.

Economic Realities

The economic plan for the American household has seen a profound change. Three decades ago, females often gravitated toward academic departments such as English, literature, foreign language, and fine arts. Women now are either the heads of household or part of a working couple. They have as strong or stronger interest than men in career-focused college majors. In fact, in many professional fields of study, women outnumber men.

Technology

Technology has made information readily available. There is less need to be a subject expert and greater need to be a problem solver who can operate in creative ways. Today's graduate must know how to find, analyze, synthesize, and apply information to problem solving. Computer skills have become a critical part of any quality education.[9] Students know this and want more emphasis on process skills rather than on information gathering.

Entrepreneurial Climate

Individuals are trading jobs for ownership of their own business in record numbers. Entrepreneurship is attracting college graduates with a wide range of backgrounds in business, management, technology, medicine, and hospitality. Most of these graduates share a strong desire to stakeout new territory in order to have more direct control over their work lives. Especially in the start-up phase, they need a broad range of work skills to succeed.

Lack of Common Morality

Education has historically played a role as a moral compass. Educational philosophers talk about a shared morality. Today, there is little common morality to share. Values and ethical decision-making have become a subjective matter rather than an objective standard. We are moving from a majority-based sense of what is morally correct to an individual-conscience morality.

View of Shared Heritage
Education was once used for assimilation of diverse cultures into the "American Way," but now it is more frequently about celebrating our diversity.

Each of these factors has led to change in what students expect from their college education. In the next section you will see how these factors have affected the way students look at prospective colleges.

The New Selection Process

Today's students have a different view of education. They are more centered on end goals than on the steps involved in earning a degree. Although some "old" criteria still apply when searching for a college, they often resurface in a new form and are driven by new purposes and new objectives. This section reviews each of these new selection filters.

Undergraduate Enrollment
Contrary to popular belief, total enrollment is not as important as the number of undergraduate students on a campus. Graduate and undergraduate programs often function as two separate institutions. A college or university with a disproportionate share of graduate students will often have programs, policies, and a cost structure skewed in the direction of the graduate programs, which offer more prestige, better research opportunities, and attract "star" faculty. This emphasis can be at the expense of the undergraduate program.

An undergraduate enrollment that is too big will almost certainly mean that some of your classes will be taught by visiting instructors, or by graduate students who sometimes lecture or teach under the guidance of a faculty member.[10] On the flip side, if the number of the undergraduates is too small, the resources needed for a good education may not be available.

The ideal enrollment size will vary according to the needs of a particular student; however, one ideal is an undergraduate enrollment big enough to have true diversity and full resources, yet small enough for individualized attention.[11] A good size is in the range of 2,000 to 10,000 undergraduates.

Proximity to a Major City
The size of the community in which a college is located is a major concern; however, not for the same reason it was in the past. For earlier generations, size of the community impacted how comfortable you were with the setting. Today, it is important that you look for a community that can provide adequate opportunities. A large city or metropolitan area will provide the most volunteer, cooperative, internship, externship, and permanent job-placement opportunities.

It will also bring working professionals into the classroom as adjunct professors, mentors, and guests. These opportunities will have a dramatic impact on your professional career development.[12] As an added bonus, large cities will also provide a larger number of cultural and entertainment options—bringing world class general education experiences to life.

Admission Standards

The selectivity of an institution's admission process is a concern for most students. Top-tier colleges often accept fewer than 10 - 20 percent of the students who apply. This is true even though they have a highly-motivated, credential-heavy, multi-talented group of applicants. The great majority of students, including many above-average performers, need to look at schools that are not as selective as these top colleges.

You want a college that will value you—recognize your unique talents and your special needs. It is important that you be viewed as a whole, instead of merely as scores on an exam. Colleges that are about helping individuals succeed have such a view of their applicants.

College Costs

The total cost of an education can be the pivotal decision point. With discounting and financial aid from outside sources dramatically reducing the true tuition rate, you should be able to find a college you can afford utilizing available grants, one annual loan, and reasonable monthly payments. An expensive college may be a great college choice, but it is not worth bankrupting your future. Affordable alternatives are out there.

When calculating the true cost of a college education, it is important to remember opportunity costs, which are in addition to the direct costs of tuition, fees, and room and board. Opportunity cost is the lost income and missed experience resulting from your time in college. Lost income makes the average time to graduation one of the most important criteria when considering a college. On the other hand, keep reminding yourself of the long-term income you'd lose by not going to college at all.

Average Financial Aid Award

While tuition rate is important, the critical number is the amount you must pay after discounts. These discounts are called institutional scholarships or grants. It is important to look at the average scholarship/grant amount awarded to students at a specific college and the percent of students that get this aid.

Retention to Graduation

Graduation rates demonstrate more than student commitment. They also measure the services offered in the areas of academic advising, financial aid, student life, support services, and the quality of classroom instruction. A better measure of student persistence is retention from year one to year two. Between the first two years, transferring is less costly and students are still in a shopping mode. It is a good test of consumer satisfaction.

Student Diversity

The world becomes more of a cultural melting pot every day. This is especially true as the main economic engines become more international. A college that reflects this diversity in its student makeup provides a much more realistic educational experience. We all learn from each other, and we learn more about the real world from people who are somewhat different from us in background and culture. Look for a college that offers a diverse student population mix. Employers feel that students from this type of college experience are better employee candidates.[13]

Placement Services

The Placement Department should be one of your first stops in visiting a campus. It is a critical service you are paying for when you select a college. These departments counsel and help prepare students for the job search campaign and assist them in acquiring job experiences while still enrolled. These services include providing opportunities for internships, co-op work experiences, and part-time jobs. The placement results of a college are critical, especially for graduates in your major field of interest; however, a good basic indicator of service is the ratio of full-time placement counselors to students enrolled. This will give you a look at the institution's commitment to job placement and other work related education opportunities.

Enrollment Growth

A simple measure of a college's current standing with the public and its viability is its annual change in enrollment. Except for top, highly selective colleges that intentionally hold enrollment, a college that has flat or declining numbers may lack the services and resources necessary to support its customers—the students. A growing college at least shows some market acceptance. You need to ask yourself, "If more people are going to college each year, why isn't the enrollment increasing at this school?"

Program Strengths

Because you are paying for an education, it only makes sense that your college major should be a leading determinant in college selection. If a college specializes in, and has a large percent of its enrollment in areas that are important to you, you can be confident that the college will allocate sufficient resources to these programs. Would you go to a shoe store to buy CD's? Know what you want and go to a college that specializes in it.

Control Status

Check whether a particular college is not-for-profit or for-profit. There are some good for-profit schools; however, at a for-profit school, part of your tuition will be used to pay taxes and to return profit to investors. At a not-for-profit school, this is not the case; all of your tuition must, by law, be spent on your education. A for-profit school must clearly be a better choice for you to warrant spending some of your precious educational dollars on investor profits and taxes.

Average Class Size

The average class size at a college will give you a good idea of the amount and type of interaction you can expect from your instructors. If possible, you should get the average class size for your proposed major or department. While little evidence exists to support the position that small classes are better, very few students report that they prefer larger classes. Look for programs with average class sizes under 35.

Majors Available

The match of majors available at a college with your chosen field is very important. It is such an important selection factor, that the next section, "Selecting a College Major is Critical," is devoted to this topic.

General Education

A strong general education component is very important even in an applied degree program. Built into the general education component and articulated to all of the career-focused courses should be a strong emphasis on the development of speaking, writing, and technology skills.

Early Skills Development

While your plan may be to finish your bachelor's degree, you never know when and why you might be side-tracked. A good program of applied study should allow you to exit your program at the end of the first, second, or third year with marketable career skills. Look for a program that does not save all of the career coursework for the final two years. It should also allow you to exit and reenter school without loss of credit or continuity.

Advisory System

The advisory system should make you feel as though the college is centered on you—the customer. Students should have frequent contact with their advisor. The advisor should be able to answer your questions and know where to send you when they can't. They should also be available at any reasonable time of day and make you feel as though you are a priority and not a chore.

Selecting a College Major

Your major field of study should be at the root of your decision when choosing a college. Many students select a college without giving full consideration to their future major or field of study. This can be dangerous!

Determining your major is a huge decision; it's often easier to think in terms of a first and a second major choice. Then it's important to select a college that offers both of these choices. Once assured you have found such a college, you have gone a long way toward making a good college choice. You need to consider colleges that offer your top choice, as well as possible alternatives, because you, like many other students, may change majors while in college. If a change in major requires changing colleges, the cost of your degree goes up dramatically. In most cases, such a change will require additional time to graduation, and that means extra college costs and lost earnings.

Size, location, cost, and placement services are important considerations when selecting a college, but these are really secondary to your major field selection. The education you receive in your area of study is the product you are buying. It will determine, to a great extent, the value of your degree at graduation and in the job market.

Today's Job Market

The job market for today's new college graduates is still strong. This results in great job opportunities as well as increased starting salaries. In some areas of the country and in some fields, there are early signs of labor shortages. At the same time, this good news is tempered by the fact that the spread between college graduates getting the best job offers and those getting lesser ones is getting much larger. This can be measured by the number of offers received, quality of initial job responsibilities, and starting salaries offered. While computer engineers had average starting salaries of over $46,000 per year in 1999, graduates entering Social Science related jobs had average salaries of $29,000.[14]

Narrowing Your Choices

Before selecting a major, you need to determine what you want from your field of study in terms of education and career results. Answering the following questions will help you narrow your choice from the long list of available majors. If nothing else, it should at least point you to families of related majors that best fit your personal profile.

- **Achievements and Prior Academic Preparation.** Have you taken a realistic look at your past academic record to determine if you have the ability for a particular field of study?
- **Career Expectations.** Do you have career expectations that are in line with what this major typically delivers?
- **Goals You Have for Your Education.** What do you expect your education to do for you?
- **Lifestyle and Current Personal Commitments.** How will this major impact your life commitments in terms of intensity of study and time required to earn the desired credential?
- **Personal Interests and Attitudes.** Do your interests seem to match well with the required coursework?
- **Top Major Choices.** Sometimes your long-term, always-wanted-to-be ideas are best. What is it that you wanted to be when you grew up?

Six Clusters of Majors

In this book, fields of study are grouped based on shared characteristics into one of six families or clusters, as shown on the following page. While most books group fields of study according to job/career tracks or academic disciplines, the clusters presented here share characteristics related to the skills required, background needed, and outcomes expected. For example, in the Analytical/Computational cluster, majors are highly structured, detail-oriented, based on logic and problem solving, and require a great deal of work with numbers. Within each cluster, majors can take varying amounts of time to complete. Some majors are usually offered as associate degree programs while others are at the bachelor or graduate school level.

Where the Jobs Are

A recent study of job offers made to new college graduates found that 80 percent of all offers were in the fields of business, engineering and computer science.[15] This means most job-offers are in fields related to majors in the Applied Quantitative, Analytical/Computational and Quantitative clusters. If career advancement and job prospects are a critical concern for you, then you should give serious consideration to selecting a major from these three clusters.

Applied Quantitative	Analytical/ Computational	Quantitative
Aerospace Engineering	Accountancy	Biochemistry
Agriculture	Actuarial Science	Biology
Architectural Engineering	Business Administration	Botany
Architecture	Criminal Justice & Admin.	Chemistry
Chemical Engineering	Commerce	Dental/Pre-Dental
Civil Engineering	E-Commerce	Earth Science
Computer Applications	Computer Networks	Ecology
Computer Science	Computer Programming	EEG Technology
Computer Aided Drafting	Computer Systems	Fitness Technology
Electrical & Computer Engineering	Consumer Economics	General Science
Electrical Engineering	Economics	Geology
Engineering Mechanics	Environmental Design	Health Sciences
Engineering Science	Finance	Mathematics
Engineering Technology	Health Service Mgmnt	Medical Assistant
Environment Control Tech.	Hotel Management	Meteorology
Environmental Health Engineering	Institutional Admin.	Microbiology
Information Sciences	International Business	Natural Science
Material Science Engineering	Law	Nuclear Medicine Tech.
Math & Computer Science	Management	Nursing
Mechanical Engineering	Marketing	Optometry
Metallurgical Engineering	Medical Records	Pharmacy
Mining Engineering	Operations Research	Physical/Corrective Therapy
Naval Science	Paralegal	Physical Science
Nuclear Engineering	Securities & Financial Analysts	Physics
Petroleum Engineering	Telecommunications	Pre Medical
		Pre Professional, Other
		Radiology Technology
		Respiratory Therapy
		Surgical Technology
		Veterinarian/Pre-Veterinarian
		Zoology

Social Sciences	Verbal	Fine Arts
American Studies	Arts & Letters - General	Advertising
Anthropology	Arts & Letters - Honors	Art
Black Studies	Classical Languages (Greek)	Art Design
Childcare Studies	Classical Languages (Latin)	Art History
Education - Elementary	Communication Arts	Art Studio
Education - Secondary	English	Arts Pre Professional Studies
Education - Specialist	Journalism	
Geography	Literature	Communications & Theatre
Government	Modern & Classical Language	
History	Modern & Foreign Language	Dance
History & Philosophy of Science	Modern Languages - Arabic	Fashion Design
	Modern Languages - Chinese	Film Study
Home Economics	Modern Languages - French	Fine Arts
Hospitality & Recreation	Modern Languages - German	General Studies
International Studies	Modern Languages - Italian	Graphic Art & Design
Medical Assisting	Modern Languages - Russian	Interior Design
Medieval Studies	Modern Languages - Spanish	Music Education
Military Science	Interdisciplinary Studies	Music-Instrumental
Occupational Therapy		Music-Vocal
Physical Education		Parks, Recreation, & Leisure Studies
Political Science		
Psychiatric Social Work		Philosophy
Psychology		Speech & Drama
Recreational Therapy		Web Design
Social Work		
Social Work Assisting		
Sociology		
Theology		
Travel		
Women Studies		

Evaluating Personal Needs

While the selection criteria discussed previously are appropriate for most students, some students have unique needs that present important considerations in the college selection process. They include:

A. Learning Style

B. Personality Type

C. Aptitudes, Strengths, and Weaknesses

D. College Experience Expectations

E. Personal Commitment

Learning Style

There is more to education than likes and dislikes. You may choose a major that appeals to you, but if you don't have the ability to study in this field, for whatever reason, you will become frustrated, gain little, and waste much. On the other hand, if the education matches your learning style, but is only of marginal interest to you, you will at least be gaining something and moving forward. *Learning styles* are a popular concept today. They are related to the different ways each of us acquire and apply knowledge.

Some of us learn best through what we hear, others by what we read; some of us require a great deal of individual attention, while others learn best when given independent assignments. Every major can accommodate different learning styles. It is important that you look beyond just your interests to see how well a college major will accommodate your learning style. You need to be sure that your college choice offers an educational plan that allows you to capitalize on your learning style strengths.

Some of the basic continuums of learning styles are as follows:

- *Structured vs. Spontaneous Planning*—Is the program tightly structured or open to independent exploration and flexible enough to accommodate individual needs?
- *Interactive vs. Static Presentations*—Does the course work allow for classroom interaction with faculty or is it lecture based?
- *Comprehensive vs. Progressive Approach*—Is the course work approached from a predetermined plan or does it progress in response to student interest?
- *Independent vs. Group Dynamic Study*—Is group work and discussion encouraged or is independent study the norm?
- *Focused vs. Global View*—Does the curriculum take a shotgun approach to topics or a highly focused view?

A good education program will combine opportunities to learn from all of these approaches.

Personality Type

Closely related to an individual's learning style is his or her personality type. While personality differences should not hinder the learning process, the proper fit between your disposition and the flavor of the college will go a long way toward making your college experience more positive and enjoyable. A college's "personality" can be hard to gauge, but it is worth the effort. Visit the college, view students' interactions, and meet with your potential classmates. Profiles presented by the admission staff or in guidebooks are often dressed-up versions of the campus created by the marketing staff and may not paint a totally accurate picture. Find out for yourself.

Aptitudes, Strengths, and Weaknesses

Your aptitudes and strengths should play a big part in your selection process. They are more significant than previously thought in the matching process. Most deficiencies can be remediated with appropriate work and course planning, but many colleges fail to consider your aptitudes and strengths and don't provide the proper opportunities for growth. These opportunities might include: honors programs, enrichment offerings, special internships, opportunities to work one-on-one with faculty, local opportunities outside the college, and adequate advanced-level coursework.

College Experience Expectations

In an earlier section, you read about evaluating your major expectations. Equally important are the expectations you have for your college experience in general. When you have a realistic understanding of these expectations, and take the time to determine whether a particular college has what you want, you will be increasing your chances of success.

Personal Commitment

After learning styles, personal commitment is the second most important special need to consider. The majority of students have to balance college with a number of other commitments that range from family responsibilities and work to a commitment to a region or city. Your college of choice must be convenient and flexible enough to change as your personal situation changes. It should offer programs at several levels from certificate and associate degrees to bachelor degrees. You should gain marketable skills throughout your program of study so that you can leave before graduation and still build a career based on specific competencies. In all cases, you should have the option of an accelerated time to degree.

By giving serious consideration to personal needs, you will eliminate a number of colleges from your list and be closer to making a good choice.

What Makes a College Ideal for You?

Career Development

As mentioned previously, one of the primary reasons students report for attending college is career and job development. Many colleges have responded to this demand by developing strong career service departments. Placement services for students should be more than just an add-on at the end of the program; they should be an integral part of the curriculum and the total education experience from the first day of enrollment. This service should include opportunities for cooperative education, internships, externships, work place visits, work-study, practitioner-based instruction, part-time job opportunities, and finally, assistance in acquiring permanent, professional full-time positions. It is also important that these opportunities be convenient to campus or your home, and that your college have a strong placement reputation in the surrounding business community.

When it comes time for permanent job placement, individual counseling can be very important in the job search. The college must have a big enough professional placement staff to serve the number of undergraduate and graduate students normally seeking their services.

The best career and job opportunities will be found in and near large metropolitan areas, where a diverse economy can provide a wide range of job placement or advancement options and training while still in college.

Major

No college is strong in all subject areas. The ideal college for you will be strong in your principal major of interest. While a college's general reputation is important for ranking the overall institution, a more important consideration is its reputation in your major field of study.[16] One way to determine a specific college's strength is by the sheer size of a school or department within a college. Most colleges will put more resources where they have more students.

While developing your major, you may have reasons for wanting to step out and then back into college. A solid program should give you the option of stepping out with some marketable skills at various stages in your education. A program that saves all the major course work until the end of the degree program will not provide such an option. Ask friends, relatives, and potential employers about a college's reputation in a specific field.

Technology

As technology drives business, it will also drive education. All of the information in the world is now readily available to any student with access to the Internet. A good college choice will use this technology throughout the college experience in every course. The days of providing students with the information, formulas, and materials they will need in their future job have quickly become obsolete. A college must be a technology service center rather than an information filter. The process of learning how to learn is now much more important than the accumulation of facts.

Cost

No school, no matter how good, is a sound choice unless you can afford it. Tuition alone does not make up the true cost of education, since most colleges and many other agencies provide financial aid for students. The bottom line to be concerned with is the gap between the tuition charged and aid received. You should be comfortable with the size of this gap.

Time to Degree

Closely related to affordability is the opportunity to graduate in a reasonable time frame. Such a schedule will allow you to enter the workforce sooner and begin earning income and experience, while other students, not in such a program, are still paying tuition.

Convenience
A good choice will be convenient to your way of life. The school should be a reasonable distance from your home or workplace, offer classes when you are available to take them and allow you to get from class to class with ease.

Secret Indicators for Selecting a College

Certain indicators, which are readily available but often overlooked, will help you determine the best college for you. These are "secret" only because most people don't talk about them. They apply when evaluating all but the very elite colleges and universities.

Growth
You should look for stable, and hopefully, growing enrollment. A college with declining enrollment is probably not meeting the demands of the quickly changing marketplace of potential students.

Emphasis
The average class size should be small enough for frequent interaction with other students and instructors, but large enough for a diversity of ideas. Look for a college that is instruction-based, rather than research-centered. This means, shop for a school that values instruction over an emphasis on publishing and research by its faculty. Research-based universities are not poor choices, but you need to know that at these institutions many senior faculty will be preoccupied with their own projects, thus taking time away from teaching and counseling activities.

A high percent of instruction delivered by teaching assistants can make even the biggest name college mediocre.

Facilities
The overall physical appearance of the campus is a good measure of the college's attention to detail. The condition of the college facilities will also give you some gauge of the college's financial position. When was the last building on campus built or renovated, and what is the current condition of existing structures?

Don't be impressed with pictures of proposed new facilities. Buildings in the planning phase are probably too far off to serve you while you are enrolled. If the campus is not well maintained, the school may be having financial difficulties. This may mean that shortfalls will arise in other service areas as well.

Scholarships
The relative size of the average student aid award as measured against the tuition rate, will demonstrate the college's commitment to helping the recruited

student. Ask how institutional aid distribution decisions are made and what your chances are of receiving any.

Majors

Determine whether majors are available from the three clusters on p. 13; these areas provide over 80 percent of the job opportunities and, by far, the highest average starting salaries for new graduates.

Student Needs

A college with a high transfer-in rate means the "sophisticated buyer" or student who has previous college experience finds it attractive. These students have been at other schools and know what was missing and important for them to find.

A retention rate that is high in comparison to other similar colleges demonstrates that the currently enrolled students are satisfied with the service levels and programs of the institution. This rate should be available to you by major area of study.

Materials

Overly-slick admission materials might be masking a problem with program quality and indicate a school's need to use ploys, rather than facts, as the primary recruiting tool. Colleges should be willing to provide you with access to the campus and to the information that answers most of your questions. The best way to find out for yourself is a campus visit.

Campus Visit

While you are on campus, observe items that give you an indication of the college's suitability. As you walk through buildings, you should look at the classrooms to see whether the facilities are updated. At many colleges, the buildings may not be modern, but the technology in the classrooms and the general environment should be inviting and exciting with plenty of available computers and other resources. You should take time to visit the placement department to see if they post job opportunities or if cooperative-related opportunities are available for students in your field of study.

As you arrive on campus, you need to answer a number of questions: Is there a nearby public transportation center? Is parking adequate during the times you will be on campus—day or evening? Is there evidence of interaction between senior faculty and students, or do most students seem to move through a series of lectures and then on to predominantly "student-only" meeting places? Are the student recreation facilities, athletic fitness centers, and bookstore modern and busy? Do you see signs of tutoring and group study? When evaluating a college look for every indicator you can think of. Don't merely depend on conventional measures of quality.

How the Best "201" Were Selected

The colleges featured in this book are those that respond to current student demand. While community colleges do an outstanding job in delivering quality education, only public, private, and proprietary colleges and universities offering baccalaureate degree programs were considered. A computer model was designed and loaded with data from one or more of the following sources:

- Public information from national database sources
- Institutional surveys
- Institutional web sites and publications

The colleges and universities were evaluated in five summary areas:

1. Opportunity for the general student population to get into and pay for a college.
2. The relative success of previous classes in graduating in a timely fashion.
3. The commitment made by the school to develop career opportunities.
4. The overall college experience.
5. Recent market response to the college or university.

Within each of these broad categories, specific criteria were reviewed. They included the following items, shown along with their weight factor:

Criteria	Weight
1. Share of Majors in Applied Fields	15
2. Population of the Surrounding Cities	15
3. Admissions Selectivity	12
4. Institutional Commitment to Job Placement Services	12
5. Freshman Graduating in 4-years or less	10
6. Unique Program Offerings for "Non-traditional" Students	10
7. Diversity of Student Population	7
8. Annual Change in Undergraduate Enrollment	7
9. Availability of Technology	7
10. Job Placement Rate	7
11. Annual Tuition Rate for In-state Students	5
12. Freshmen Retention Rate	5
13. Percent of Courses Taught by Practitioners	5
14. Commitment to Capital Improvements on Campus	4
15. Average Institutional Financial Aid as a % of Tuition	3
16. Percent of Students Receiving Institutional Aid	2
17. Size of Undergraduate Enrollment	2

Within each criteria, several different scores were possible, which when multiplied by the criteria weight produced an item score. The item scores were summed to arrive at a cumulative overall index for each college. Each measurement used the most current available data. In most cases, this was from the 2000-01 or 2001-02 academic year.

The schools with the 201 highest index scores were selected for additional analysis and compilation and finally for presentation in the college profile section. Several of the criteria items were combined to arrive at each of the five summary scores which are represented by the 1-5 star system.

Colleges are listed alphabetically by state.

How to Use the College Profile Sheets

While there are many sources of information on colleges and universities, the profile sheets highlight items identified in this book as critical to the selection process. As you narrow your choices, you should go directly to the colleges and universities that interest you to get primary source data from Internet sites or institutional publications. This section explains the main tools available on the college profile pages of this book.

Note: Listed tuition rates for public universities reflect in-state tuition.

How Does it Compare?

This section gives you a quick one (★) to five-star (★★★★★) evaluation of a school in five key areas—this evaluation is in comparison to other colleges identified in this book:

- **College Experience:** A comparison of the total college experience.
- **Market Response:** This indicator reports on how other students have viewed this college in terms of its responsiveness to basic student needs and trends.
- **Chance of Getting Out:** Compares this college to others in the study on their relative rate of success in getting students to graduation in a timely fashion.
- **Chance of Getting In:** Gives you an indication of the likelihood of today's "average profile" student getting in.
- **Career Development Potential:** A measurement of an institution's commitment to your overall career preparation and development.

WEAK	BELOW AVERAGE	AVERAGE	ABOVE AVERAGE	EXCEPTIONAL
★	★★	★★★	★★★★	★★★★★

Total Cost

This item gives you a view of the true cost of attending the institution. It considers both the average time to graduation and the tuition rate. The evaluation of "average" is in comparison to other colleges identified in this book rather than to any national or regional averages.

Most Popular Areas of Study

This item relates the top major choices of current students at this institution to the clusters identified the section on "Selecting a College Major." You'll also find a list of the school's top individual majors.

Unique Features

These are special programs or opportunities the school offers to help meet the needs of the "non-traditional" student who makes up today's largest student segment.

Endnotes

[1] "Earnings Continue to Rise for College Graduates," Facts in Brief, Higher Educ. and Nat'l Affairs, American Council on Education, January 17, 2000, Vol. 49, No. 1.

[2] L. J. Sax, A. W. Astin, W.S., Korn, K. M. Mahoney, "The American Freshman: National Norms for Fall 1999," Higher Education Research Institute, UCLA, p. 50.

[3] P. Eckel, M. Green, B. Hill, W. Mallon, "Taking Charge of Change: A Primer for Colleges and Universities," On Change II, p. 3-4.

[4] Arthur Levine and Jeanette S. Cureton, "Collegiate Life: An Obituary," Change, May/June 1998, p. 14-51.

[5] Lisa Kartus, "Gaining by Degrees," University Business, Feb. 2000, p. 40-59.

[6] "Shifts in the Composition of Student Aid," State of Diffusion, The Institute of Higher Policy, August 1999.

[7] Charles Dervarics, "Senators Question College Costs," Black Issues in Higher Education, March 16, 2000, Vol. 17, No. 2, p. 7.

[8] Rachel E. Silverman, " Employers Face Dearth of IT Workers As Demand Exceeds Supply, Data Show," Wall Street Journal, Monday, April 10, 2000, p. A2.

[9] "Computers Now Required at Michigan State," Black Issues in Higher Education, March 2, 2000, Vol. 16, No. 27, p. 43.

[10] Meg McSherry Breslin, " Trend Toward Temporary Faculty Worries University of Illinois," Chicago Tribune, April 9, 2000, Section 4, p. 2.

[11] Jack B. Schrum, "Democracy's Last Stand: The Role of the New Urban University," Texas Wesleyan University, 1999, p. 76.

[12] Andrew J. Cannon, Mark J. Arnold, "Student Expectations of Collegiate Internship Programs in Business: A 10-Year Update," Journal of Education for Business, March 1998, Vol. 73, No. 4, p. 202-205.

[13] "Survey Reveals Strong Support for Diversity in Ed, Business," Higher Educ. and Nat'l Affairs, American Council on Education, Feb. 28, 2000, Vol. 49, #4, p. 1.

[14] "JobTrak.Com Index Job Listings," February 2000.

[15] "Proportion of Offers by Curricular Area," Salary Survey, National Association of Colleges and Employers, April 1998, Vol. 37, Issue 2, p. 7.

[16] George Dehne, "Think Small," University Business, Mar. 2000, Vol. 3, #2, p. 25.

ARE THE COLLEGES IN THIS BOOK RIGHT FOR YOU?

Take a minute to answer the following questions to determine how well the colleges profiled in this book will meet your need. If you answer "yes" to 5 or more questions, this book is worth reviewing. If you answer "yes" to 8 or more, this book is an essential tool for your college search.

	Yes	No
1. Is career development or securing a good job among the most important reasons for attending college?	☐	☐
2. Do you need to juggle your college education with other commitments such as work, family, and friends?	☐	☐
3. Is the true cost of your education a critical factor in your college selection process?	☐	☐
4. Do you plan to graduate in four years or less?	☐	☐
5. Are you hoping to study a subject area that has the greatest number of job opportunities after graduation?	☐	☐
6. Do you plan to incorporate career development activities like internships and externships into your education?	☐	☐
7. Should people working as practitioners in the field you are studying teach some of your courses?	☐	☐
8. Do you expect college advising to be readily available and to be a help in all facets of your life?	☐	☐
9. Do you expect to have opportunities for world class cultural experiences while you are in college?	☐	☐
10. Is applied course work more appealing than research-based work?	☐	☐

Alabama State University
915 South Jackson Street
Montgomery, AL 36101
www.alasu.edu, (334) 229-4100

COLLEGE PROFILE
Tuition 2002-2003: $2,904
Average Freshman Institutional Aid Award: $3,088
Percent of Students who Receive Freshman Institutional Aid Award: 10%
Average Student Loan: $3,406
Undergraduate Enrollment - Fall 2001: 4,711
Average Class Size: 30
Demographics of Student Body: African-American 90%, Caucasian 9%
Percent of Students with Transfer-in Credit: 4%
Special Adult Programs: Yes

HOW DOES IT COMPARE?
College Experience: ★★★
Market Response: ★★
Chance of Getting Out: ★★
Chance of Getting In: ★★★★★
Career Development Potential: ★★★
Total Cost: Low Tuition
Longer than Average Time to Graduation

MOST POPULAR AREAS OF STUDY
Major Clusters: Social Sciences, Analytical/Computational
Most Popular Majors: Computer Information Systems 40%, Education 35%, Biology 21%

UNIQUE FEATURES
— Alabama State University's Business and Technology Center gives students a one-stop shop for management resources in the Information Age. The Center offers students help with software training, consulting services on what hardware and software to buy, video conferencing, opinion polling, R&D surveys, customer satisfaction research, or assistance with preparing proposals for government contracts, they can help.

— Louis Stokes Alabama Alliance for Minority Participation Program (LSAAMP) — A six week program for college-bound graduating high school seniors who plan to major in science, engineering, math, chemistry, computer science, biology, physics or science education; $1,000 stipend for qualified students.

Auburn University — Montgomery

PO Box 244023
Montgomery, AL 36123
www.aum.edu, (334) 244-3000

COLLEGE PROFILE
Tuition 2002-2003: $3,210
Average Freshman Institutional Aid Award: $2,800
Percent of Students who Receive Freshman Institutional Aid Award: 32%
Average Student Loan: $3,971
Undergraduate Enrollment - Fall 2001: 4,166
Average Class Size: 20
Demographics of Student Body: African-American 34%, Asian 2%, Caucasian 63%, Hispanic 1%
Percent of Students with Transfer-in Credit: 52%
Special Adult Programs: Yes

HOW DOES IT COMPARE?
College Experience: ★★★
Market Response: ★★
Chance of Getting Out: ★★
Chance of Getting In: ★★★
Career Development Potential: ★★★
Total Cost: Low Tuition
Average Time to Graduation

MOST POPULAR AREAS OF STUDY
Major Clusters: Analytical/Computational, Social Sciences
Most Popular Majors: Business/Marketing 33%, Computer Information 25%, Protective Services 10%

UNIQUE FEATURES
— Offers students a unique mix of quality, convenience, affordability, and prestige. Key advantages are AUM's strong academic programs, active campus life, metropolitan location, and convenient scheduling (including evenings and weekends).

— Students benefit from small classes, access to advanced computer technology, and opportunities for research, internships, and other practical experiences.

Birmingham-Southern College

900 Arkadelphia Road
Birmingham, AL 35254
www.bsc.edu, (205) 226-4600

COLLEGE PROFILE
Tuition 2002-2003: $17,650
Average Freshman Institutional Aid Award: $6,000
Percent of Students who Receive Freshman Institutional Aid Award: 84%
Average Student Loan: $3,276
Undergraduate Enrollment - Fall 2001: 1,347
Average Class Size: 17
Demographics of Student Body: White 87%, African-American 8%, Asian 3%, Other 2%
Percent of Students with Transfer-in Credit: 12%
Special Adult Programs: No

HOW DOES IT COMPARE?
College Experience: ★★★★
Market Response: ★★
Chance of Getting Out: ★★★
Chance of Getting In: ★★★
Career Development Potential: ★★★
Total Cost: High Tuition
Shorter than Average Time to Graduation

MOST POPULAR AREAS OF STUDY
Major Clusters: Analytical/Computational, Social Sciences
Most Popular Majors: Business Marketing 41%, Interdisciplinary/Multi Studies 11%, Biology/Life Science 6%

UNIQUE FEATURES
—The most distinctive part of the Birmingham-Southern experience is the Interim Term, a four-week period each January in which students develop their potential for creative activity and independent study by exploring one topic or interest. This intensive program of experiential learning—the middle section of the College's 4-1-4 academic calendar—offers students unique opportunities to be further enriched through on- and off- campus projects, independent study or research, foreign study experiences, and challenging and unusual internships.

—The college offers all students mentor and practical internship experience opportunities through its Interim Term, Mentor Program, and Contact Learning Program.

Stillman College

3601 Stillman Blvd.
Tuscaloosa, AL 35401
www.stillman.edu, (205) 349-4240

COLLEGE PROFILE

Tuition 2002-2003: $7,374
Average Freshman Institutional Aid Award: $5,323
Percent of Students who Receive Freshman Institutional Aid Award: 18%
Average Student Loan: $2,421
Undergraduate Enrollment - Fall 2001: 1,530
Average Class Size: 20
Demographics of Student Body: African-American 98%, Caucasian 2%
Percent of Students with Transfer-in Credit: 5%
Special Adult Programs: Yes

HOW DOES IT COMPARE?

College Experience:	★★★★
Market Response:	★★
Chance of Getting Out:	★★★★
Chance of Getting In:	★★★★★
Career Development Potential:	★★★★★
Total Cost:	Low Tuition
	Longer than Average Time to Graduation

MOST POPULAR AREAS OF STUDY

Major Clusters:	Analytical/Computational, Social Sciences
Most Popular Majors:	Business Management 47%, Social Science 18%, Biological Sciences 12%

UNIQUE FEATURES

Stillman College has made outstanding strides in providing students and faculty with the latest, cutting-edge technology. These strides were recognized when Apple Computers awarded the Leadership in Technology Award to the college. Stillman is among very few institutions nationwide that simultaneously are using a fiber optic network and wireless access

Troy State University — Montgomery

231 Montgomery Street
Montgomery, AL 36103
www.tsum.edu, (334) 241-9506

COLLEGE PROFILE
Tuition 2002-2003: $3,020
Average Freshman Institutional Aid Award: $0
Percent of Students who Receive Freshman Institutional Aid Award: 0%
Average Student Loan: $2,402
Undergraduate Enrollment - Fall 2001: 2,696
Average Class Size: 20
Demographics of Student Body: African-American 43%, Asian 2%, Caucasian 52%, Hispanic 2%
Percent of Students with Transfer-in Credit: 37%
Special Adult Programs: Yes

HOW DOES IT COMPARE?
College Experience: ★★★
Market Response: ★★★
Chance of Getting Out: ★★
Chance of Getting In: ★★★★
Career Development Potential: ★★★
Total Cost: Low Tuition
Longer than Average Time to Graduation

MOST POPULAR AREAS OF STUDY
Major Clusters: Analytical/Computational, Social Sciences
Most Popular Majors: Business Management 58%, Psychology 14%, Social Sciences 10%

UNIQUE FEATURES
—TSUM is an adult evening institution catering to the needs of the adult learner. The typical TSUM student works full-time, has family responsibilities, and attends TSUM on a part-time basis. TSUM recognizes the needs, motivations, and time constraints of the adult learner.

—The average age of TSUM's students is 28 and the minority enrollment is about 43% of the student body. The school offers some classes during the lunch hour and on weekends. Many students find it more convenient to take courses via television, the Internet, or by individual learning contracts, which allow students to work at their own disciplined pace with faculty assistance.

Get In. Get Out. Get a Job. // 29

University of Alabama — Tuscaloosa

739 University Blvd.
Tuscaloosa, AL 35487
www.ua.edu, (205) 348-6010

COLLEGE PROFILE
Tuition 2002-2003: $3,555
Average Freshman Institutional Aid Award: $6,759
Percent of Students who Receive Freshman Institutional Aid Award: 63%
Average Student Loan: $4,135
Undergraduate Enrollment - Fall 2001: 15,201
Average Class Size: 23
Demographics of Student Body: African-American 15%, Asian 1%, Caucasian 81%, Hispanic 1%
Percent of Students with Transfer-in Credit: 66%
Special Adult Programs: Yes

HOW DOES IT COMPARE?
College Experience: ★★★★
Market Response: ★★
Chance of Getting Out: ★★★★
Chance of Getting In: ★★★
Career Development Potential: ★★★
Total Cost: Low Tuition
              Average Time to Graduation

MOST POPULAR AREAS OF STUDY
Major Clusters: Analytical/Computational, Verbal
Most Popular Majors: Business Management 28%, Communications 10%, Education 9%

UNIQUE FEATURES
—For over a decade, The University of Alabama has been one of the top public flagship universities in the Southeast in enrollment of African-American students. Enrollment of African-American students in UA's Graduate School has increased by 38.5 percent since 1996.

—The University of Alabama College of Engineering has received an endowment of more than $8 million from the estate of Alton N. Scott. The bequest is the largest gift ever given to the College of Engineering, and the second largest estate gift in the history of the University.

University of Alabama — Birmingham

1530 3rd Avenue South
Birmingham, AL 35294
www.uab.edu, (205) 934-4011

COLLEGE PROFILE
Tuition 2002-2003: $3,880
Average Freshman Institutional Aid Award: $8,134
Percent of Students who Receive Freshman Institutional Aid Award: 49%
Average Student Loan: $3,792
Undergraduate Enrollment - Fall 2001: 9,954
Average Class Size: 28
Demographics of Student Body: African-American 30%, Asian 3%, Caucasian 60%, Hispanic 1%
Percent of Students with Transfer-in Credit: 50%
Special Adult Programs: Yes

HOW DOES IT COMPARE?
College Experience: ★★★
Market Response: ★★★
Chance of Getting Out: ★★★
Chance of Getting In: ★★★★
Career Development Potential: ★★★
Total Cost: Low Tuition
              Longer than Average Time to Graduation

MOST POPULAR AREAS OF STUDY
Major Clusters: Quantitative, Social Sciences
Most Popular Majors: Biology 7%, Psychology 6%, Communications 4%

UNIQUE FEATURES

— UAB was established in 1969 as an autonomous university within the University of Alabama system. It now serves as one of the nation's top ranked universities in research support, higher education and provider of world-class medical care.

— UAB Options/Services for Adult Students is designed to meet the needs of degree-seeking adult students whose life circumstances require an alternative approach to educational opportunities

University of Mobile
PO Box 13220
Mobile, AL 36663
www.umobile.edu, (251) 675-5990

COLLEGE PROFILE
Tuition 2002-2003: $8,940
Average Freshman Institutional Aid Award: $3,130
Percent of Students who Receive Freshman Institutional Aid Award: 14%
Average Student Loan: $4,290
Undergraduate Enrollment - Fall 2001: 1,802
Average Class Size: 17
Demographics of Student Body: African-American 22%, Caucasian 62%, Hispanic 1%, Native American 1%
Percent of Students with Transfer-in Credit: 14%
Special Adult Programs: Yes

HOW DOES IT COMPARE?
College Experience: ★★★
Market Response: ★★★
Chance of Getting Out: ★★★
Chance of Getting In: ★★★★★
Career Development Potential: ★★★
Total Cost: Average Tuition
                     Average Time to Graduation

MOST POPULAR AREAS OF STUDY
Major Clusters: Quantitative, Social Sciences
Most Popular Majors: Interdisciplinary Studies 18%
                     Education 17%, Health Professions 15%

UNIQUE FEATURES
—The University of Mobile has developed its Adult Degree Completion Program to meet the needs of adult students who are 25 or older who have two or more years of college credit. These students are typically working full-time and are interested in completing their degrees in the evening while continuing to work. The opportunity is provided to begin classes at different times of the year and attend class one night per week on a year-round basis, thus allowing an earlier completion of the degree.

—The Continuing Education Department seeks to meet the needs of Mobile area businesses and the public in general by offering non-credit courses in areas of expressed public interest. The venue of these courses may be on the University of Mobile campus or on a client's premises.

DeVry University — Phoenix

2149 W. Dunlap Avenue
Phoenix, AZ 85021
www.devry-phx.edu, (602) 870-9222

COLLEGE PROFILE
Tuition 2002-2003: $9,390
Average Freshman Institutional Aid Award: $2,735
Percent of Students who Receive Freshman Institutional Aid Award: 3%
Average Student Loan: $5,942
Undergraduate Enrollment - Fall 2001: 3,050
Average Class Size: 24
Demographics of Student Body: African-American 6%, Asian 6%, Caucasian 68%, Hispanic 15%, Native American 5%
Percent of Students with Transfer-in Credit: 8%
Special Adult Programs: Yes

HOW DOES IT COMPARE?
College Experience: ★★★
Market Response: ★★
Chance of Getting Out: ★★
Chance of Getting In: ★★★★★
Career Development Potential: ★★★
Total Cost: Average Tuition
Shorter than Average Time to Graduation

MOST POPULAR AREAS OF STUDY
Major Clusters: Applied Quantitative
Most Popular Majors: Computer & Information Sciences 51%, Electronics 49%

UNIQUE FEATURES
Three-semesters per academic year for earlier graduation; class schedules designed for full-time or part-time workers; and morning, afternoon, evening, weekend and online courses.

Philander Smith College
812 W. 13th Street
Little Rock, AR 72202
www.philander.edu, (501) 375-9845

COLLEGE PROFILE
Tuition 2002-2003: $4,056
Average Freshman Institutional Aid Award: $650
Percent of Students who Receive Freshman Institutional Aid Award: 9%
Average Student Loan: $1,280
Undergraduate Enrollment - Fall 2001: 859
Average Class Size: 17
Demographics of Student Body: African-American 95%, Caucasian 1%, Hispanic 1%
Percent of Students with Transfer-in Credit: 12%
Special Adult Programs: Yes

HOW DOES IT COMPARE?
College Experience: ★★★
Market Response: ★★
Chance of Getting Out: ★★
Chance of Getting In: ★★★★
Career Development Potential: ★★★
Total Cost: Low Tuition
 Longer than Average Time to Graduation

MOST POPULAR AREAS OF STUDY
Major Clusters: Analytical/Computational, Social Sciences
Most Popular Majors: Business Management 47%, Education 15%, Social Sciences 11%

UNIQUE FEATURES
Management Institute offers adults the opportunity to finish their degrees with a major in organizational management. Students attend class one night per week for a minimum of 17 months to complete the core requirements for the major in organizational management.

California State University — Fresno

5241 N. Maple Ave.
Fresno, CA 93740
www.csufresno.edu, (559) 278-4240

COLLEGE PROFILE
Tuition 2002-2003: $7,666
Average Freshman Institutional Aid Award: $2,070
Percent of Students who Receive Freshman Institutional Aid Award: 53%
Average Student Loan: $2,691
Undergraduate Enrollment - Fall 2001: 15,413
Average Class Size: 27
Demographics of Student Body: African-American 5%, Asian 12%, Caucasian 38%, Hispanic 28%, Native American 1%
Percent of Students with Transfer-in Credit: 51%
Special Adult Programs: Yes

HOW DOES IT COMPARE?
College Experience: ★★★★
Market Response: ★★★★★
Chance of Getting Out: ★★★★
Chance of Getting In: ★★★★
Career Development Potential: ★★★★
Total Cost: Average Tuition
Longer than Average Time to Graduation

MOST POPULAR AREAS OF STUDY
Major Clusters: Verbal, Analytical/Computational
Most Popular Majors: Liberal Arts & Sciences 25%,
Business Management 15%,
Social Sciences 10%

UNIQUE FEATURES
Fresno State and IBM recently announced an agreement to deploy leading-edge business and learning technology solutions at California State University, Fresno. IBM will provide technology and train faculty and students in e-business solutions to enable the University to consult with and nurture local businesses.

California State University — San Bernardino
5500 University Parkway
San Bernardino, CA 92407
www.csusb.edu, (909) 880-5000

COLLEGE PROFILE
Tuition 2002-2003: $1,733
Average Freshman Institutional Aid Award: $1,556
Percent of Students who Receive Freshman Institutional Aid Award: 44%
Average Student Loan: $2,100
Undergraduate Enrollment - Fall 2001: 11,019
Average Class Size: 19
Demographics of Student Body: African-American 11%, Asian 7%, Caucasian 37%, Hispanic 29%
Percent of Students with Transfer-in Credit: 48%
Special Adult Programs: Yes

HOW DOES IT COMPARE?
College Experience: ★★★★
Market Response: ★★
Chance of Getting Out: ★★
Chance of Getting In: ★★★★
Career Development Potential: ★★★
Total Cost: Low Tuition
              Average Time to Graduation

MOST POPULAR AREAS OF STUDY
Major Clusters: Analytical/Computational, Social Sciences
Most Popular Majors: Liberal Studies 16%, Accounting 4%, Criminal Justice 4%

UNIQUE FEATURES
—Cal State is distinguished as the only Inland Empire university with prestigious national accreditation for its College of Business and Public Administration.

—Because of recent growth, new facilities (10 new buildings in 10 years) have been established, providing students, faculty and staff with an excellent learning and working environment equipped with superior technological capabilities.

DeVry University — Pomona
901 Corporate Center Drive
Pomona, CA 91768
www.pom.devry.edu, (909) 622-8866

COLLEGE PROFILE
Tuition 2002-2003: $9,950
Average Freshman Institutional Aid Award: $8,250
Percent of Students who Receive Freshman Institutional Aid Award: 1%
Average Student Loan: $7,066
Undergraduate Enrollment - Fall 2001: 3,669
Average Class Size: n/a
Demographics of Student Body: African-American 8%, Asian 34%, Caucasian 22 %, Hispanic 31%, Native American 1%
Percent of Students with Transfer-in Credit: n/a
Special Adult Programs: n/a

HOW DOES IT COMPARE?
College Experience: ★★
Market Response: ★★★
Chance of Getting Out: ★★
Chance of Getting In: ★★★★★
Career Development Potential: ★★
Total Cost: Average Tuition
Average Time to Graduation

MOST POPULAR AREAS OF STUDY
Major Clusters: Analytical/Computational, Applied Quantitative
Most Popular Majors: Computer & Information Sciences 43%, Telecommunications 40%, Electronics 19%

UNIQUE FEATURES
—For students pursuing internships and work opportunities, the many businesses in the Los Angeles area provide for excellent work opportunities.

—Career Development course covers key aspects of conducting a successful job search, such as creating resumes, researching prospective employers, and gaining valuable interviewing practice.

Fresno Pacific University

1717 S. Chestnut Avenue
Fresno, CA 93702
www.fresno.edu, (559) 453-2000

COLLEGE PROFILE
Tuition 2002-2003: $16,200
Average Freshman Institutional Aid Award: $4,197
Percent of Students who Receive Freshman Institutional Aid Award: 98%
Average Student Loan: $5,677
Undergraduate Enrollment - Fall 2001: 878
Average Class Size: 20
Demographics of Student Body: African-American 2%, Asian 4%, Caucasian 65%, Hispanic 19%, Native American 1%
Percent of Students with Transfer-in Credit: 80%
Special Adult Programs: Yes

HOW DOES IT COMPARE?
College Experience: ★★★★★
Market Response: ★★★★
Chance of Getting Out: ★★
Chance of Getting In: ★★
Career Development Potential: ★★
Total Cost: High Tuition
Shorter than Average Time to Graduation

MOST POPULAR AREAS OF STUDY
Major Clusters: Analytical/Computational, Social Sciences
Most Popular Majors: Business Management 39%, Education 34%, Theological Studies 4%

UNIQUE FEATURES
The CRC is designed to help students make wise career decisions—help them set career goals, choose a major, and develop an effective job search strategy. To accomplish this the CRC will guide students through the four steps of career development: Self assessment, Career exploration, Goal setting, and Job search.

Golden Gate University
536 Mission Street
San Francisco, CA 94105
www.ggu.edu, (415) 442-7000

COLLEGE PROFILE
Tuition 2002-2003: $9,600
Average Freshman Institutional Aid Award: $3,385
Percent of Students who Receive Freshman Institutional Aid Award: 64%
Average Student Loan: $7,069
Undergraduate Enrollment - Fall 2001: 1,015
Average Class Size: 15
Demographics of Student Body: African-American 9%, Asian 13%, Caucasian 43%, Hispanic 8%
Percent of Students with Transfer-in Credit: 90%
Special Adult Programs: Yes

HOW DOES IT COMPARE?
College Experience: ★★★★
Market Response: ★★★★★
Chance of Getting Out: ★★★
Chance of Getting In: ★★★
Career Development Potential: ★★★★
Total Cost: Average Tuition
                       Average Time to Graduation

MOST POPULAR AREAS OF STUDY
Major Clusters: Analytical/Computational, Applied Quantitative
Most Popular Majors: Business Management 72%,
                       Computer & Information Sci. 17%, Psychology 4%

UNIQUE FEATURES
Golden Gate offers day, evening and weekend courses year round at campuses throughout California. Students may attend classes at multiple locations if they want, or earn their degree or certificate either partially or entirely online through their nationally recognized CyberCampus.

Holy Names College
3500 Mountain Blvd.
Oakland, CA 94619
www.hnc.edu, (510) 436-1000

COLLEGE PROFILE
Tuition 2002-2003: $18,150
Average Freshman Institutional Aid Award: $8,545
Percent of Students who Receive Freshman Institutional Aid Award: 56%
Average Student Loan: $2,625
Undergraduate Enrollment - Fall 2001: 506
Average Class Size: 12
Demographics of Student Body: African-American 34%, Asian 8%, Caucasian 24%, Hispanic 15%
Percent of Students with Transfer-in Credit: 72%
Special Adult Programs: Yes

HOW DOES IT COMPARE?
College Experience: ★★★★
Market Response: ★★★
Chance of Getting Out: ★★
Chance of Getting In: ★★★★
Career Development Potential: ★★★
Total Cost: High Tuition
              Average Time to Graduation

MOST POPULAR AREAS OF STUDY
Major Clusters: Quantitative, Analytical/Computational
Most Popular Majors: Business 28%, Psychology 14%, Liberal Arts 13%

UNIQUE FEATURES
— Holy Names Colleges has built great relationships with businesses, government, and the arts—providing students access to internships and job opportunities.

— Interdisciplinary Care program is central to the general education curriculum.

John F. Kennedy University

12 Altarinda Road
Orinda, CA 94563
www.jfku.edu, (925) 254-0200

COLLEGE PROFILE
Tuition 2002-2003: $11,610
Average Freshman Institutional Aid Award: $1,000
Percent of Students who Receive Freshman Institutional Aid Award: 80%
Average Student Loan: $6,000
Undergraduate Enrollment - Fall 2001: 196
Average Class Size: 20
Demographics of Student Body: African-American 12%, Asian 4%, Caucasian 66%, Hispanic 7%, Native American 3%
Percent of Students with Transfer-in Credit: 100%
Special Adult Programs: Yes

HOW DOES IT COMPARE?
College Experience: ★★
Market Response: ★
Chance of Getting Out: ★★
Chance of Getting In: ★★★★
Career Development Potential: ★★★★
Total Cost: Average Tuition
Average Time to Graduation

MOST POPULAR AREAS OF STUDY
Major Clusters: Verbal, Analytical/Computational
Most Popular Majors: Liberal Arts 63%, Business Management 25%
Psychology 12%

UNIQUE FEATURES

— JFKU was one of the first institutions in the United States dedicated solely to adult education.

— JFKU recently announced its new linked sport psychology program that allows students to save time and money by concurrently getting their master's degree in sport psychology and doctorate in clinical psychology (PsyD). This program is on the cutting edge of the relatively new field of sport psychology, and it is one of only a few such programs at an accredited university.

Loyola Marymount University
One LMU Drive
Los Angeles, CA 90045
www.lmu.edu, (310) 338-2700

COLLEGE PROFILE
Tuition 2002-2003: $20,342
Average Freshman Institutional Aid Award: $6,410
Percent of Students who Receive Freshman Institutional Aid Award: 43%
Average Student Loan: $3,051
Undergraduate Enrollment - Fall 2001: 5,144
Average Class Size: 17
Demographics of Student Body: African-American 6%, Asian 12%,
    Caucasian 48%, Hispanic 17%, Native American 1%
Percent of Students with Transfer-in Credit: 4%
Special Adult Programs: Yes

HOW DOES IT COMPARE?
College Experience:	★★★★
Market Response:	★★★★★
Chance of Getting Out:	★★★
Chance of Getting In:	★
Career Development Potential:	★★★
Total Cost:	High Tuition
	Shorter than Average Time to Graduation

MOST POPULAR AREAS OF STUDY
Major Clusters:	Analytical/Computational, Verbal
Most Popular Majors:	Business Management 26%, English 15%
	Communications 14%

UNIQUE FEATURES
—ENCORE Adult Reentry Degree Program is Loyola Marymount University's reentry program designed for adults 25 years and older who wish to begin college or resume an interrupted college education.

—Study Abroad Programs spur about 20 countries or regions.

Mount St. Mary's College
12001 Chalon Road
Los Angeles, CA 90049
www.msmc.la.edu, (310) 954-4000

COLLEGE PROFILE
Tuition 2002-2003: $18,782
Average Freshman Institutional Aid Award: n/a
Percent of Students who Receive Freshman Institutional Aid Award: n/a
Average Student Loan: n/a
Undergraduate Enrollment - Fall 2001: 1,708
Average Class Size: 20
    Caucasian 19%, Hispanic 43%
Percent of Students with Transfer-in Credit: 90%
Special Adult Programs: Yes

HOW DOES IT COMPARE?
College Experience: ★★★★
Market Response: ★★★★★
Chance of Getting Out: ★★★
Chance of Getting In: ★
Career Development Potential: ★★★★
Total Cost: High Tuition
                  Shorter than Average Time to Graduation

MOST POPULAR AREAS OF STUDY
Major Clusters: Quantitative, Analytical/Computational
Most Popular Majors: Health Professions 29%, Liberal Arts 18%
                        Business Management 15%

UNIQUE FEATURES
— Students choose Mount St. Mary's College because of its small size, excellent academic reputation, and alumnae working in key positions in health care, business, and education.

— Approximately 75 percent of the MSMC science majors who apply to medical schools gain acceptance; over 90 percent of MSMC science majors who apply to graduate programs other than medical school are accepted into programs of their choice. Recent graduates attend Mayo School of Medicine, Harvard, Johns Hopkins, UCLA, UCI, NYU, Northwestern, Tulane, USC and UCSF, among others.

National University
11255 N. Torrey Pines Road
La Jolla, CA 92037
www.nu.edu, (800) NAT-UNIV

COLLEGE PROFILE
Tuition 2002-2003: $7,965
Average Freshman Institutional Aid Award: $0
Percent of Students who Receive Freshman Institutional Aid Award: 0%
Average Student Loan: $4,035
Undergraduate Enrollment - Fall 2001: 5,360 Average Class Size: 20
Demographics of Student Body: African-American 13%, Asian 9%, Caucasian 52%, Hispanic 19%
Percent of Students with Transfer-in Credit: 90%
Special Adult Programs: Yes

HOW DOES IT COMPARE?
College Experience: ★★★★
Market Response: ★★
Chance of Getting Out: ★★
Chance of Getting In: ★★★★
Career Development Potential: ★★★
Total Cost: Average Tuition
                        Longer than Average Time to Graduation

MOST POPULAR AREAS OF STUDY
Major Clusters: Analytical/Computational, Social Sciences
Most Popular Majors: Business Management 21%,
                        Computer & Information Sciences 20%,
                        Psychology 19%,

UNIQUE FEATURES
— NU has ranked in the "Top 100" of colleges and universities awarding bachelor's and master's degrees to minorities in all disciplines since the U.S. Office of Education began reporting such data in 1996 through its Integrated Post-Secondary Education Data (IPEDS) Complete Survey.

— NU recommends more teachers and is one of the foremost suppliers of kindergarten through 12th-grade teachers in the state.

San Francisco State University

1600 Holloway Avenue
San Francisco, CA 94132
www.sfsu.edu, (334) 229-4100

COLLEGE PROFILE
Tuition 2002-2003: $1,826
Average Freshman Institutional Aid Award: $7,343
Percent of Students who Receive Freshman Institutional Aid Award: 35%
Average Student Loan: $5,806
Undergraduate Enrollment - Fall 2001: 20,166
Average Class Size: 24
Demographics of Student Body: African-American 6%, Asian 33%, Caucasian 25%, Hispanic 13%
Percent of Students with Transfer-in Credit: 59%
Special Adult Programs: Yes

HOW DOES IT COMPARE?
College Experience: ★★★
Market Response: ★★★
Chance of Getting Out: ★★★
Chance of Getting In: ★★★★
Career Development Potential: ★★★★
Total Cost: Low Tuition
Average Time to Graduation

MOST POPULAR AREAS OF STUDY
Major Clusters: Analytical/Computational, Social Sciences
Most Popular Majors: Business Management 22%, Social Sciences 11%
Visual and Performing Arts 9%

UNIQUE FEATURES
— Through the College of Extended Learning's Open University program, the public can take regular University classes without formal admission to SFSU. In addition, Extended Learning offers hundreds of classes each year for professional development and personal enrichment.

— The SFSU Motto is *Experentia Docet*—Experience Teachers. Programs emphasize hands-on-learning through credit-earning internships and more than 100 community-focused centers and institutes.

San Jose State University
One Washington Square
San Jose, CA 95192
www.sjsu.edu, (408) 924-1000

COLLEGE PROFILE
Tuition 2002-2003: $1,909
Average Freshman Institutional Aid Award: $1,502
Percent of Students who Receive Freshman Institutional Aid Award: 32%
Average Student Loan: $2,526
Undergraduate Enrollment - Fall 2001: 20,711
Average Class Size: 28
Demographics of Student Body: African-American 4%, Asian 40%, Caucasian 24%, Hispanic 15%
Percent of Students with Transfer-in Credit: 13%
Special Adult Programs: N/A

HOW DOES IT COMPARE?
College Experience: ★★
Market Response: ★★
Chance of Getting Out: ★★
Chance of Getting In: ★★★★
Career Development Potential: ★★★
Total Cost: Low Tuition
Longer than Average Time to Graduation

MOST POPULAR AREAS OF STUDY
Major Clusters: Analytical/Computational, Applied Quantitative
Most Popular Majors: Business Management 30%, Engineering 11%, Visual & Performing Arts 7%

UNIQUE FEATURES
Silicon Valley firms and agencies seek SJSU students for internships, summer work programs and for assistance with research and development projects. Silicon Valley firms employ more graduates from SJSU than from any other university in the nation.

Sonoma State University
1801 East Cotati Avenue
Rohnert Park, CA 94928
www.sonoma.edu, (707) 664-2880

COLLEGE PROFILE
Tuition 2002-2003: $2,226
Average Freshman Institutional Aid Award: $1,471
Percent of Students who Receive Freshman Institutional Aid Award: 24%
Average Student Loan: $3,976
Undergraduate Enrollment - Fall 2001: 6,278
Average Class Size: 21
Demographics of Student Body: African-American 2%, Asian 5%,
 Caucasian 64%, Hispanic 10%, Native American 1%
Percent of Students with Transfer-in Credit: 12%
Special Adult Programs: Yes

HOW DOES IT COMPARE?
College Experience:	★★★★
Market Response:	★★★★
Chance of Getting Out:	★★★★
Chance of Getting In:	★★★★
Career Development Potential:	★
Total Cost:	Low Tuition
	Longer than Average Time to Graduation

MOST POPULAR AREAS OF STUDY
Major Clusters:	Analytical/Computational, Social Sciences
Most Popular Majors:	Business 18%, Liberal Arts 11%, Psychology 11%

UNIQUE FEATURES
— SSU has a commitment to graduating students who have the ability to think critically and ethically and can effectively use information technology.

— The Jean and Charles Schulz Information Center is one of the most modern and unique college libraries in the country. This $42 million structure, which opened last fall, contains a modern catalog retrieval system that makes access to the more than 600,00 volumes and 12,000 print and online journals and one million microform items as easy as possible for students.

The National Hispanic University
14271 Story Road
San Jose, CA 95127
www.nhu.edu, (408) 254-6900

COLLEGE PROFILE
Tuition 2002-2003: $3,200
Average Freshman Institutional Aid Award: $1,452
Percent of Students who Receive Freshman Institutional Aid Award: 53%
Average Student Loan: $3,688
Undergraduate Enrollment - Fall 2001: 341
Average Class Size: 20
Demographics of Student Body: African-American 4%, Asian 7%, Caucasian 7%, Hispanic 82%
Percent of Students with Transfer-in Credit: 20%
Special Adult Programs: Yes

HOW DOES IT COMPARE?
College Experience: ★★
Market Response: ★★★★
Chance of Getting Out: ★★★★
Chance of Getting In: ★★★★★
Career Development Potential: ★★★★★
Total Cost: Low Tuition
              Average Time to Graduation

MOST POPULAR AREAS OF STUDY
Major Clusters: Verbal, Analytical/Computational
Most Popular Majors: Liberal Arts 67%, Business Management 29%, Computer Information Sciences 5%

UNIQUE FEATURES
— The National Hispanic University is proud to be the first Hispanic University to be accredited by the Western Association of Schools and Colleges (WASC) in California

— The key features of NHU's Teacher Education Program are that all classes are at night or Saturdays; are given on a 6-week basis; 98% of NHU students pass the RICA; small class sizes.

University of California — Riverside

900 University Avenue
Riverside, CA 92521
www.ucr.edu, (909) 787-1012

COLLEGE PROFILE

Tuition 2002-2003: $4,000
Average Freshman Institutional Aid Award: $11,412
Percent of Students who Receive Freshman Institutional Aid Award: 75%
Average Student Loan: $10,863
Undergraduate Enrollment - Fall 2001: 12,714
Average Class Size: n/a
Demographics of Student Body: African-American 6%, Asian 41%, Caucasian 26%, Hispanic 22%
Percent of Students with Transfer-in Credit: 24%
Special Adult Programs: Yes

HOW DOES IT COMPARE?

College Experience: ★★★
Market Response: ★★★★★
Chance of Getting Out: ★★★★★
Chance of Getting In: ★★★★
Career Development Potential: ★★
Total Cost: Low Tuition
                   Average Time to Graduation

MOST POPULAR AREAS OF STUDY

Major Clusters: Quantitative, Analytical/Computational
Most Popular Majors: Business Management 25%, Social Sciences 19%, History 19%

UNIQUE FEATURES

— The UCR/UCLA Program in Biomedical Sciences offers an accelerated track to obtaining both the B.S. and M.D. degrees. The UCR Division of Biomedical Sciences and the UCLA School of Medicine offer it jointly. It trims the traditional eight years required for a B.A./B.S. and M.D. education to seven years. The shortened path to a medical degree is the only program of its kind in California. It draws some of the best and brightest pre-medical students to the UCR campus.

— Nationally renowned Teacher Education and Education Doctorate programs are available.

University of San Francisco

2130 Fulton Street
San Francisco, CA 94117
www.usfca.edu, (415) 422-5555

COLLEGE PROFILE

Tuition 2002-2003: $21,660
Average Freshman Institutional Aid Award: $9,796
Percent of Students who Receive Freshman Institutional Aid Award: 57%
Average Student Loan: $5,962
Undergraduate Enrollment - Fall 2001: 4,733
Average Class Size: 21
Demographics of Student Body: African-American 6%, Asian 17%, Caucasian 44%, Hispanic 9%, Native American 1%
Percent of Students with Transfer-in Credit: 41%
Special Adult Programs: Yes

HOW DOES IT COMPARE?

College Experience: ★★★★
Market Response: ★★★★★
Chance of Getting Out: ★★★
Chance of Getting In: ★★
Career Development Potential: ★★★
Total Cost: High Tuition
              Shorter than Average Time to Graduation

MOST POPULAR AREAS OF STUDY

Major Clusters: Analytical/Computational, Quantitative
Most Popular Majors: Business Management 9%, Nursing 7%, Computer & Information Sciences 7%

UNIQUE FEATURES

— The Freshman Resource Center is for all first year students who have questions or concerns about anything related to academics or university life.

— The Freshman Programs Coordinator develops and coordinates enrichment programs for freshmen that promote the successful completion of their first year at USF. It has an open door policy, so students are welcome to drop by at any time.

— USF's Freshman Advantage seminars are a perfect starting place for new students. These seminars are courses designed specifically for Freshmen. They cover a wide range of interesting topics and are taught by faculty members excited about the subject and eager to educate and inspire you.

National American University — Colorado Springs

5125 N. Academy Blvd.
Colorado Springs, CO 80918
www.national.edu, (719) 277-0588

COLLEGE PROFILE
Tuition 2002-2003: $9,600
Average Freshman Institutional Aid Award: $0
Percent of Students who Receive Freshman Institutional Aid Award: 0%
Average Student Loan: $4,790
Undergraduate Enrollment - Fall 2001: 325
Average Class Size: n/a
Demographics of Student Body: African-American 22%, Asian 4%, Caucasian 57%, Hispanic 4%
Percent of Students with Transfer-in Credit: 60%
Special Adult Programs: Yes

HOW DOES IT COMPARE?
College Experience: ★★★
Market Response: ★★
Chance of Getting Out: ★★
Chance of Getting In: ★★★★
Career Development Potential: ★★★★
Total Cost: Average Tuition
Shorter than Average Time to Graduation

MOST POPULAR AREAS OF STUDY
Major Clusters: Analytical/Computational, Applied Quantitative
Most Popular Majors: Business Management 74%, Computer & Information Sciences 26%

UNIQUE FEATURES
Whether you are a traditional college student, adult or distance learner, NAU offers you the caring, supportive, student service oriented environment with all the tools to help you succeed.

National American University — Denver

1325 S. Colorado Blvd. #100
Denver, CO 80222
www.national.edu, (303) 758-6700

COLLEGE PROFILE
Tuition 2002-2003: $8,865
Average Freshman Institutional Aid Award: $0
Percent of Students who Receive Freshman Institutional Aid Award: 0%
Average Student Loan: $4,035
Undergraduate Enrollment - Fall 2001: 380
Average Class Size: 12
Demographics of Student Body: African-American 5%, Asian 6%, Caucasian 61%, Hispanic 7%
Percent of Students with Transfer-in Credit: 70%
Special Adult Programs: Yes

HOW DOES IT COMPARE?
College Experience: ★★★
Market Response: ★★
Chance of Getting Out: ★★
Chance of Getting In: ★★★★
Career Development Potential: ★★★★
Total Cost: Average Tuition
Shorter than Average Time to Graduation

MOST POPULAR AREAS OF STUDY
Major Clusters: Analytical/Computational, Applied Quantitative
Most Popular Majors: Business Management 90%,
Computer & Information Sciences 10%

UNIQUE FEATURES
The Denver campus offers flexible schedules and accessible degree programs in business and computers designed for today's world of business.

University of Colorado — Colorado Springs

1420 Austin Bluffs Parkway
Colorado Springs, CO 80933
www.uccs.edu, (719) 262-3000

COLLEGE PROFILE
Tuition 2002-2003: $3,257
Average Freshman Institutional Aid Award: $2,031
Percent of Students who Receive Freshman Institutional Aid Award: 36%
Average Student Loan: $3,908
Undergraduate Enrollment - Fall 2001: 4,967
Average Class Size: 25
Demographics of Student Body: African-American 4%, Asian 6%, Caucasian 77%, Hispanic 9%
Percent of Students with Transfer-in Credit: 41%
Special Adult Programs: Yes

HOW DOES IT COMPARE?
College Experience: ★★★
Market Response: ★★
Chance of Getting Out: ★★
Chance of Getting In: ★★★
Career Development Potential: ★★★★
Total Cost: Low Tuition
Longer than Average Time to Graduation

MOST POPULAR AREAS OF STUDY
Major Clusters: Social Sciences, Analytical/Computational
Most Popular Majors: Social Sciences/History 20%,
Business Management 18%
Psychology 15%

UNIQUE FEATURES
Most recently, the University Center was expanded, and the school built a new $28 million El Pomar Center, which houses the library. The new library is almost triple the size of the old library. The new library has seating for 1,300 students, has 33 group study rooms, 3 teleconferencing rooms, and 280 personal computers.

… … … … … … … … … … … … … …
University of Colorado — Denver
PO Box 173364. Campus Box 151
Denver, CO 80217
www.cudenver.edu, (303) 556-2400

COLLEGE PROFILE
Tuition 2002-2003: $2,934
Average Freshman Institutional Aid Award: $4,303
Percent of Students who Receive Freshman Institutional Aid Award: 26%
Average Student Loan: $5,188
Undergraduate Enrollment - Fall 2001: 6,474
Average Class Size: 26
Demographics of Student Body: African-American 5%, Asian 11%, Caucasian 67%, Hispanic 11%, Native American 1%
Percent of Students with Transfer-in Credit: 59%
Special Adult Programs: n/a

HOW DOES IT COMPARE?
College Experience: ★★★★
Market Response: ★★★★
Chance of Getting Out: ★★★
Chance of Getting In: ★★★
Career Development Potential: ★★★
Total Cost: Low Tuition
Longer than Average Time to Graduation

MOST POPULAR AREAS OF STUDY
Major Clusters: Analytical/Computational, Quantitative
Most Popular Majors: Business Management 19%, Biological Sciences 7%, Psychology 6%

UNIQUE FEATURES
— With both day and evening courses, students can tailor their schedules to meet their employment and personal needs. With CU-Denver's location in the heart of Denver's dynamic lower downtown, students have access to all the cultural, professional, and recreational amenities that Denver has to offer.

— The Career Center at CU-Denver offers a full array of services. Students are assisted in choosing a major, selecting a career path, gaining experience, developing job search skills, and finding a job upon graduation.

University of Denver
University Park
Denver, CO 80208
www.du.edu, (303) 871-2000

COLLEGE PROFILE
Tuition 2002-2003: $22,680
Average Freshman Institutional Aid Award: $8,196
Percent of Students who Receive Freshman Institutional Aid Award: 79%
Average Student Loan: $5,807
Undergraduate Enrollment - Fall 2001: 3,467
Average Class Size: 20
Demographics of Student Body: African-American 3%, Asian 5%, Caucasian 85%, Hispanic 6%, Native American 1%
Percent of Students with Transfer-in Credit: 19%
Special Adult Programs: Yes

HOW DOES IT COMPARE?
College Experience: ★★★
Market Response: ★★★★
Chance of Getting Out: ★★★
Chance of Getting In: ★
Career Development Potential: ★★
Total Cost: High Tuition
              Shorter than Average Time to Graduation

MOST POPULAR AREAS OF STUDY
Major Clusters: Analytical/Computational, Verbal
Most Popular Majors: Business Management 37%, Communications 13%, Social Sciences 12%

UNIQUE FEATURES
— The University is investing more than $350 million in new and refurbished buildings as part of a plan to unite all university programs on the University Park campus by fall 2003.

— Ninety-eight nations are represented in the University of Denver's student body. Non-U.S. citizens comprise 7.41 percent of UD's student population.

University of Southern Colorado
2200 Bonforte Blvd.
Pueblo, CO 81001
www.uscolo.edu, (719) 549-2100

COLLEGE PROFILE
Tuition 2002-2003: $2,450
Average Freshman Institutional Aid Award: $1,526
Percent of Students who Receive Freshman Institutional Aid Award: 17%
Average Student Loan: $4,365
Undergraduate Enrollment - Fall 2001: 5,303
Average Class Size: n/a
Demographics of Student Body: African-American 5%, Asian 2%,
   Caucasian 60%, Hispanic 23%, Native American 1%
Percent of Students with Transfer-in Credit: 9%
Special Adult Programs: n/a

HOW DOES IT COMPARE?
College Experience: ★★
Market Response: ★★★★
Chance of Getting Out: ★★★
Chance of Getting In: ★★★★★
Career Development Potential: ★★
Total Cost: Low Tuition
              Average Time to Graduation

MOST POPULAR AREAS OF STUDY
Major Clusters: Social Sciences, Analytical/Computational
Most Popular Majors: Social Sciences 32%, Business Management 15%
                      Computer & Information Sciences 8%

UNIQUE FEATURES
The University of Southern Colorado scored second in the state in this year's college report cards hitting its marks in a wide range of areas such as graduation rate, retention rates, minority enrollment and low per-student administrative costs.

Albertus Magnus College
700 Prospect Street
New Haven, CT 06511
www.albertus.edu, (203) 773-8550

COLLEGE PROFILE
Tuition 2002-2003: $15,204
Average Freshman Institutional Aid Award: $4,500
Percent of Students who Receive Freshman Institutional Aid Award: 69%
Average Student Loan: $2,625
Undergraduate Enrollment - Fall 2001: 1,872
Average Class Size: 18
Demographics of Student Body: African-American 19%, Asian 1%,
    Caucasian 72%, Hispanic 7%, Native American 1%
Percent of Students with Transfer-in Credit: 15%
Special Adult Programs: Yes

HOW DOES IT COMPARE?
College Experience: ★★★
Market Response: ★★★★
Chance of Getting Out: ★★★★
Chance of Getting In: ★★
Career Development Potential: ★★★
Total Cost: High Tuition
                    Shorter than Average Time to Graduation

MOST POPULAR AREAS OF STUDY
Major Clusters: Analytical/Computational, Social Sciences
Most Popular Majors: Business Management 67%, Social Sciences 13%,
                       Sociology 8%

UNIQUE FEATURES
— Continuing Education Program is available.

—Accelerated Degree Completion students take 10 courses per year,
2 per 8-week module, meeting twice a week in the evening for 2 1/2 hours per night, earning 30 total credits.

— All classrooms are hi-tech and all students' seats are computer-ready. All classrooms have Internet connections.

Central Connecticut State University

1615 Stanley Street
New Britain, CT 06050
www.ccsu.edu, (860) 832-3200

COLLEGE PROFILE
Tuition 2002-2003: $2,314
Average Freshman Institutional Aid Award: $5,711
Percent of Students who Receive Freshman Institutional Aid Award: 44%
Average Student Loan: $2,891
Undergraduate Enrollment - Fall 2001: 9,551
Average Class Size: 25
Demographics of Student Body: African-American 6%, Asian 3%, Caucasian 72%, Hispanic 5%
Percent of Students with Transfer-in Credit: 35%
Special Adult Programs: n/a

HOW DOES IT COMPARE?
College Experience:	★★★
Market Response:	★★★
Chance of Getting Out:	★★★
Chance of Getting In:	★★★
Career Development Potential:	★★★
Total Cost:	Low Tuition
	Longer than Average Time to Graduation

MOST POPULAR AREAS OF STUDY
Major Clusters: Analytical/Computational, Social Sciences
Most Popular Majors: Business Management 26%, Social Sciences 16%, Engineering 9%

UNIQUE FEATURES
— The Association of American Colleges & Universities declared CCSU a "Leadership Institution" — one of only 16 in the nation and the only one in Connecticut. The schools were characterized by extensive innovations in their curriculum, pedagogy, and organizational structure.

— CCSU now offers a doctorate in educational leadership, Ed.D.

Saint Joseph College
1678 Asylum Avenue
West Hartford, CT 06117
www.sjc.edu, (860) 232-4571

COLLEGE PROFILE
Tuition 2002-2003: $19,610
Average Freshman Institutional Aid Award: $8,549
Percent of Students who Receive Freshman Institutional Aid Award: 85%
Average Student Loan: $5,186
Undergraduate Enrollment - Fall 2001: 1,227
Average Class Size: 20
Demographics of Student Body: African-American 8%, Asian 2%, Caucasian 63%, Hispanic 4%
Percent of Students with Transfer-in Credit: 90%
Special Adult Programs: Yes

HOW DOES IT COMPARE?
College Experience: ★★★★
Market Response: ★★★★
Chance of Getting Out: ★★★
Chance of Getting In: ★
Career Development Potential: ★★★★
Total Cost: High Tuition
Shorter than Average Time to Graduation

MOST POPULAR AREAS OF STUDY
Major Clusters: Analytical/Computational, Quantitative
Most Popular Majors: Health Professions 22%, Psychology 14%, Home Economics 12%

UNIQUE FEATURES
The School for Young Children is one of the oldest early childhood centers in the state. The School for Young Children also serves as an on-site laboratory for preschool teacher training.

Howard University
2100 Sixth Street NW
Washington, DC 20059
www.howard.edu, (202) 806-6100

COLLEGE PROFILE
Tuition 2002-2003: $9,515
Average Freshman Institutional Aid Award: $7,166
Percent of Students who Receive Freshman Institutional Aid Award: 7%
Average Student Loan: $4,143
Undergraduate Enrollment - Fall 2001: 6,982
Average Class Size: 15
Demographics of Student Body: African-American 84%, Asian 3%, Caucasian 1%, Hispanic 1%
Percent of Students with Transfer-in Credit: 5%
Special Adult Programs: Yes

HOW DOES IT COMPARE?
College Experience: ★★★★
Market Response: ★★
Chance of Getting Out: ★★★
Chance of Getting In: ★★★★★
Career Development Potential: ★★
Total Cost: Average Tuition
Average Time to Graduation

MOST POPULAR AREAS OF STUDY
Major Clusters: Quantitative, Analytical/Computational
Most Popular Majors: Biological Sciences 11%, Performing Arts 7%, Psychology 14%

UNIQUE FEATURES
— The University owns and operates two successful broadcast properties: public television station WHUT-TV and commercial radio station WIIUR-FM.

— This year, the University opened two new 80,000 square foot digital libraries, outfitted with the latest telecommunication and audiovisual capabilities.

Southeastern University

501 I Street SW
Washington, DC 20024
www.seu.edu, (202) 488-8162

COLLEGE PROFILE
Tuition 2002-2003: $7,980
Average Freshman Institutional Aid Award: $0
Percent of Students who Receive Freshman Institutional Aid Award: 0%
Average Student Loan: $3,500
Undergraduate Enrollment - Fall 2001: 497
Average Class Size: 20
Demographics of Student Body: African-American 77%, Asian 4%, Caucasian 3%, Hispanic 1%
Percent of Students with Transfer-in Credit: 29%
Special Adult Programs: Yes

HOW DOES IT COMPARE?
College Experience: ★★
Market Response: ★★
Chance of Getting Out: ★★
Chance of Getting In: ★★★★
Career Development Potential: ★★★★
Total Cost: Average Tuition
Shorter than Average Time to Graduation

MOST POPULAR AREAS OF STUDY
Major Clusters: Analytical/Computational, Applied Quantitative
Most Popular Majors: Business Management 38%,
Computer & Information Science 30%,
Liberal Arts and Sciences 28%

UNIQUE FEATURES
— Southeastern is a University Center with a two-year university college; a four-year undergraduate program and a graduate school. The unique academic year operates on the "quadmester system," which provides students the opportunity to obtain an undergraduate or graduate degree in a shorter period of time than the usual two year or four year programs.

— The flexible class schedules offer daytime, evening and weekend courses, which are an added convenience for students who are employed or have other obligations.

Wilmington College

320 Dupont Highway
New Castle, DE 19720
www.wilmcoll.edu, (302) 328-9401

COLLEGE PROFILE

Tuition 2002-2003: $6,690
Average Freshman Institutional Aid Award: $4,464
Percent of Students who Receive Freshman Institutional Aid Award: 32%
Average Student Loan: $2,443
Undergraduate Enrollment - Fall 2001: 3,716
Average Class Size: 17
Demographics of Student Body: African-American 13%, Asian 1%, Caucasian 57%, Hispanic 1%
Percent of Students with Transfer-in Credit: 70%
Special Adult Programs: Yes

HOW DOES IT COMPARE?

College Experience:	★★★
Market Response:	★★★★★
Chance of Getting Out:	★★★★
Chance of Getting In:	★★★★★
Career Development Potential:	★★★
Total Cost:	Low Tuition
	Average Time to Graduation

MOST POPULAR AREAS OF STUDY

Major Clusters:	Analytical/Computational, Social Sciences
Most Popular Majors:	Business Management 38%, Psychology 18%
	Health Professions 13%

UNIQUE FEATURES

— The program of day, evening, and weekend classes at Wilmington College serves traditional high school graduates as well as nontraditional adult students in need of flexible scheduling. Classes are primarily offered in seven-week, fifteen-week, and weekend modular formats.

— Wilmington College generally serves commuter students.

Barry University
11300 NE 2nd Avenue
Miami, FL 33161
www.barry.edu, (800) 756-6000

COLLEGE PROFILE
Tuition 2002-2003: $18,900
Average Freshman Institutional Aid Award: $15,714
Percent of Students who Receive Freshman Institutional Aid Award: 74%
Average Student Loan: $7,293
Undergraduate Enrollment - Fall 2001: 5,907
Average Class Size: 20
Demographics of Student Body: African-American 20%, Asian 2%, Caucasian 34%, Hispanic 29%
Percent of Students with Transfer-in Credit:
Special Adult Programs: Yes

HOW DOES IT COMPARE?
College Experience: ★★★★
Market Response: ★★★★
Chance of Getting Out: ★
Chance of Getting In: ★
Career Development Potential: ★★★
Total Cost: High Tuition
                   Average Time to Graduation

MOST POPULAR AREAS OF STUDY
Major Clusters: Analytical/Computational, Social Sciences
Most Popular Majors: Business/Marketing 20%, Education 20%, Liberal Arts 16%

UNIQUE FEATURES
— With more than 60 traditional undergraduate programs, accelerated bachelor's programs designed specifically for working adults, and more than 50 graduate programs, Barry offers superb opportunities for study, networking, community service, and professional growth.

— School of Nursing has many degree options for the students to choose from including an accelerated program in Dual Nursing and MBA degrees.

Bethune Cookman College

640 Dr. Mary McLeod Bethune Blvd.
Daytona Beach, FL 32114
www.cookman.edu, (386) 481-2000

COLLEGE PROFILE
Tuition 2002-2003: $9,810
Average Freshman Institutional Aid Award: $7,000
Percent of Students who Receive Freshman Institutional Aid Award: 41%
Average Student Loan: $5,870
Undergraduate Enrollment - Fall 2001: 2,724
Average Class Size: 20
Demographics of Student Body: African-American 90%, Caucasian 2%, Hispanic 1%
Percent of Students with Transfer-in Credit: 3%
Special Adult Programs: Yes

HOW DOES IT COMPARE?
College Experience:	★★★★
Market Response:	★
Chance of Getting Out:	★★
Chance of Getting In:	★★★
Career Development Potential:	★★★
Total Cost:	Average Tuition
	Longer than Average Time to Graduation

MOST POPULAR AREAS OF STUDY
Major Clusters: Analytical/Computational, Social Sciences
Most Popular Majors: Business Management 14%, Education 7%, Criminal Justice 8%

UNIQUE FEATURES
— Bethune-Cookman College, the 6th largest of the 39-member UNCF colleges is located in the Atlantic coast city of Daytona Beach, Florida, which has a metropolitan area population of more than 165,000.

— Under the Continuing Education Program the college operates extension sites in the state: Belle Glade, Fort Pierce, Lake Wales, Sanford, West Palm Beach, a branch campus in Spuds, and an on-campus weekend college.

Florida Metropolitan University — Tampa

3319 West Hillsborough Avenue
Tampa, FL 33614
www.fmu.edu, 813-879-6000

COLLEGE PROFILE
Tuition 2002-2003: $9,360
Average Freshman Institutional Aid Award: $1,277
Percent of Students who Receive Freshman Institutional Aid Award: 1%
Average Student Loan: $4,312
Undergraduate Enrollment - Fall 2001: 971
Average Class Size: 20
Demographics of Student Body: Asian 5%, African American 23%, Caucasian 31%, Hispanic 27%
Percent of Students with Transfer-in Credit: n/a
Special Adult Programs: Yes

HOW DOES IT COMPARE?
College Experience: ★★★
Market Response: ★★
Chance of Getting Out: ★★★
Chance of Getting In: ★★★★
Career Development Potential: ★★★★★
Total Cost: Average Tuition
                    Shorter the Average Time to Graduation

MOST POPULAR AREAS OF STUDY
Major Clusters: Analytical/Computational, Social Sciences
Most Popular Majors: Business Management 40%, Protective Services 35%, Computer Information Sciences 25%

UNIQUE FEATURES
— Florida Metropolitan University (FMU) is currently one of the largest private universities in Florida. FMU, Tampa Campus traces its roots back to 1890, making it the oldest business college in the state. In response to the demand of Florida's rapidly growing population, FMU is focused on, and dedicated to, business and career education.

— The University is also dedicated to providing a personalized teaching and learning environment designed to support the personal and professional career development of qualified undergraduate and graduate students.

Florida Southern College
111 Lake Hollingsworth Drive
Lakeland, FL 33801
www.flsouthern.edu, (863) 680-4131

COLLEGE PROFILE
Tuition 2002-2003: $15,778
Average Freshman Institutional Aid Award: $6,186
Percent of Students who Receive Freshman Institutional Aid Award: 97%
Average Student Loan: $4,401
Undergraduate Enrollment - Fall 2001: 2,452
Average Class Size: 13
Demographics of Student Body: African-American 5%, Asian 1%, Caucasian 84%, Hispanic 5%
Percent of Students with Transfer-in Credit: 32%
Special Adult Programs: Yes

HOW DOES IT COMPARE?
College Experience: ★★★★
Market Response: ★★★
Chance of Getting Out: ★★
Chance of Getting In: ★★★
Career Development Potential: ★★★★
Total Cost: High Tuition
Shorter than Average Time to Graduation

MOST POPULAR AREAS OF STUDY
Major Clusters: Analytical/Computational, Social Sciences
Most Popular Majors: Business Management 23%, Education 9%, Communication 8%

UNIQUE FEATURES
— Examined Life is a new required course for first-year students at Florida Southern College. EXL 101 is a topic specific course aimed at encouraging academic excellence and fostering the well-being of incoming first-year students by improving time management, study skills, work habits, and communication skills.

— May term abroad - International travel courses lead by faculty.

Nova Southeastern University

3301 College Avenue
Fort Lauderdale, FL 33314
www.nova.edu, (954) 262-7300

COLLEGE PROFILE
Tuition 2002-2003: $13,650
Average Freshman Institutional Aid Award: $2,714
Percent of Students who Receive Freshman Institutional Aid Award: 71%
Average Student Loan: $1,889
Undergraduate Enrollment - Fall 2001: 4,009
Average Class Size: 19
Demographics of Student Body: African-American 23%, Asian 3%, Caucasian 40%, Hispanic 21%
Percent of Students with Transfer-in Credit: 40%
Special Adult Programs: n/a

HOW DOES IT COMPARE?
College Experience: ★★★
Market Response: ★★★★
Chance of Getting Out: ★★
Chance of Getting In: ★★★★★
Career Development Potential: ★★
Total Cost: High Tuition
                Average Time to Graduation

MOST POPULAR AREAS OF STUDY
Major Clusters: Analytical/Computational, Social Sciences
Most Popular Majors: Business Management 46%, Education 36%, Health Professions 8%

UNIQUE FEATURES
— The new Library, Research, and Information Technology Center is now open. It is a $43 million, state-of-the art facility that will be Florida's largest library at capacity.

— NSU awards bachelors, master's, educational specialist, doctoral, and first-professional degrees in a wide range of fields. It has an undergraduate college and graduate schools of medicine, dentistry, pharmacy, allied health, optometry, law, computer and information sciences, psychology, education, business, oceanography, and humanities and social sciences

Get In. Get Out. Get a Job. // 67

The University of Tampa
401 W. Kennedy Boulevard
Tampa, FL 33606
www.utampa.edu, (813) 253-3333

COLLEGE PROFILE
Tuition 2002-2003: $16,150
Average Freshman Institutional Aid Award: $5,760
Percent of Students who Receive Freshman Institutional Aid Award: 87%
Average Student Loan: $3,711
Undergraduate Enrollment - Fall 2001: 3,327
Average Class Size: 20
Demographics of Student Body: African-American 5%, Asian 2%, Caucasian 66%, Hispanic 9%, Native American 1%
Percent of Students with Transfer-in Credit: 46%
Special Adult Programs: Yes

HOW DOES IT COMPARE?
College Experience:	★★★★
Market Response:	★★★★
Chance of Getting Out:	★
Chance of Getting In:	★
Career Development Potential:	★★★★
Total Cost:	High Tuition
	Shorter than Average Time to Graduation

MOST POPULAR AREAS OF STUDY
Major Clusters: Analytical/Computational, Social Sciences
Most Popular Majors: Business Management 24%, Social Sciences 13%, Education 11%,

UNIQUE FEATURES
— There are no boundaries to a UT Education. Practical experience is an integral aspect of every course. Job, internship, and community service opportunities abound. In fact, there are more internship opportunities available than students to fill them.

— The University offers an MBA Program as well as a new Masters of Science in Technology and Innovation Management Program for working professionals, with evening and weekend classes.

University of North Florida

4567 St. Johns Bluff Road South
Jacksonville, FL 32224
www.alasu.edu, (904) 620-1000

COLLEGE PROFILE

Tuition 2002-2003: $2,757
Average Freshman Institutional Aid Award: $1,421
Percent of Students who Receive Freshman Institutional Aid Award: 30%
Average Student Loan: $8,070
Undergraduate Enrollment - Fall 2001: 11,617
Average Class Size: 30
Demographics of Student Body: African-American 10%, Asian 5%, Caucasian 77%, Hispanic 5%
Percent of Students with Transfer-in Credit: 66%
Special Adult Programs: Yes

HOW DOES IT COMPARE?

College Experience: ★★★
Market Response: ★★★
Chance of Getting Out: ★★★
Chance of Getting In: ★★★★
Career Development Potential: ★★★
Total Cost: Low Tuition
                Longer than Average Time to Graduation

MOST POPULAR AREAS OF STUDY

Major Clusters: Analytical/Computational, Quantitative
Most Popular Majors: Business Management 21%, Education 15%, Health Professions 13%

UNIQUE FEATURES

— To keep pace with the school's continuing growth, UNF just opened a new Fine Arts Center and broke ground on a Science and Engineering building.

— The Re-entry Program at UNF is geared to the needs of the nontraditional college-aged students who are entering college for the first time or returning to college after a significant absence.

Columbus State University
4225 University Avenue
Columbus, GA 31907
www.colstate.edu, (706) 568-2001

COLLEGE PROFILE
Tuition 2002-2003: $2,352
Average Freshman Institutional Aid Award: $1,543
Percent of Students who Receive Freshman Institutional Aid Award: 16%
Average Student Loan: $3,185
Undergraduate Enrollment - Fall 2001: 4,450
Average Class Size: 20
Demographics of Student Body: African-American 27%, Asian 2%, Caucasian 66%, Hispanic 3%, Native American 1%
Percent of Students with Transfer-in Credit: 20%
Special Adult Programs: Yes

HOW DOES IT COMPARE?
College Experience:	★★★★
Market Response:	★★
Chance of Getting Out:	★★
Chance of Getting In:	★★★★★
Career Development Potential:	★★★
Total Cost:	Low Tuition
	Average Time to Graduation

MOST POPULAR AREAS OF STUDY
Major Clusters: Applied Quantitative, Analytical/Computational
Most Popular Majors: Education 19%, Business Management 17%, Computer & Information Sciences 16%

UNIQUE FEATURES
The Adult Learning Resource Center is a gathering place and interactive group study space designed for adult learners. All students are welcome to utilize the facilities. Its main goal is to provide a place where adult learners can find a sense of connection and belonging.

Hawaii Pacific University
1166 Fort Street
Honolulu, HI 96813
www.hpu.edu, (808) 544-0200

COLLEGE PROFILE
Tuition 2002-2003: $9,850
Average Freshman Institutional Aid Award: $2,512
Percent of Students who Receive Freshman Institutional Aid Award: 10%
Average Student Loan: $3,654
Undergraduate Enrollment - Fall 2001: 6,759
Average Class Size: 25
Demographics of Student Body: African-American 9%, Asian 24%, Caucasian 34%, Hispanic 5%, Native American 5%
Percent of Students with Transfer-in Credit: 48%
Special Adult Programs: Yes

HOW DOES IT COMPARE?
College Experience: ★★★★
Market Response: ★★★
Chance of Getting Out: ★★
Chance of Getting In: ★★
Career Development Potential: ★★★
Total Cost: Average Tuition
                Average Time to Graduation

MOST POPULAR AREAS OF STUDY
Major Clusters: Analytical/Computational, Quantitative
Most Popular Majors: Business Management 49%, Health Professions 12%
                       Protective Services 10%

UNIQUE FEATURES
— HPU now offers the Associate of Science in Management (ASM) degree online using Internet and World Wide Web (WWW) technology.

— Weekend MBA for business professionals program allows the students to learn alongside leading professionals from Hawaii's economy for a more applied look at technology in the workplace. Also, the program can be completed in only 18 months.

Boise State University

1910 University Drive
Boise, ID 83725
www.boisestate.edu, (208) 426-1011

COLLEGE PROFILE
Tuition 2002-2003: $2,984
Average Freshman Institutional Aid Award: $1,378
Percent of Students who Receive Freshman Institutional Aid Award: 19%
Average Student Loan: $2,837
Undergraduate Enrollment - Fall 2001: 14,756
Average Class Size: 20
Demographics of Student Body: African-American 1%, Asian 2%,
    Caucasian 84%, Hispanic 5%, Native American 1%
Percent of Students with Transfer-in Credit: 37%
Special Adult Programs: Yes

HOW DOES IT COMPARE?
College Experience: ★★
Market Response: ★★
Chance of Getting Out: ★★
Chance of Getting In: ★★★★★
Career Development Potential: ★★★★
Total Cost: Low Tuition
                Longer than Average Time to Graduation

MOST POPULAR AREAS OF STUDY
Major Clusters: Analytical/Computational, Social Sciences
Most Popular Majors: Business Management 20%, Education 14%,
                        Social Sciences 13%

UNIQUE FEATURES

— Boise State is a metropolitan university reflecting the character of Idaho's capital city — a center of business, government, technology, and culture — and serving the needs of the state of Idaho through undergraduate and graduate programs, research and public service.

— Location on the edge of pristine wilderness influences and enhances academic programs and research, and provide unparalleled recreational opportunities.

DePaul University
1 East Jackson Blvd.
Chicago, IL 60604
www.depaul.edu, (312) 362-8000

COLLEGE PROFILE
Tuition 2002-2003: $16,500
Average Freshman Institutional Aid Award: $6,714
Percent of Students who Receive Freshman Institutional Aid Award: 72%
Average Student Loan: $2,600
Undergraduate Enrollment - Fall 2001: 13,020
Average Class Size: 24
Demographics of Student Body: African-American 12%, Asian 10%, Caucasian 58%, Hispanic 13%
Percent of Students with Transfer-in Credit: 10%
Special Adult Programs: Yes

HOW DOES IT COMPARE?
College Experience: ★★★
Market Response: ★★★★★
Chance of Getting Out: ★★★★
Chance of Getting In: ★★
Career Development Potential: ★★
Total Cost: High Tuition
                Average Time to Graduation

MOST POPULAR AREAS OF STUDY
Major Clusters: Analytical/Computational, Verbal
Most Popular Majors: Business Management 27%, Liberal Arts 18%, Computer Information Sciences 12%

UNIQUE FEATURES
— New facilities include: State-of-the-Art McGowan Science Center, 120,000 sq. ft. Ray Meyer Fitness and Recreation Center, and 3-level Student Center.

—Lincoln Park Campus, the largest, most active of DePaul's eight campuses offers a culturally-rich urban environment with 1700 students living on campus.

DeVry University — Chicago

3300 N. Campbell Avenue
Chicago, IL 60618
www.chi.devry.edu, (773) 929-8500

COLLEGE PROFILE
Tuition 2002-2003: $9,500
Average Freshman Institutional Aid Award: $6,508
Percent of Students who Receive Freshman Institutional Aid Award: 1%
Average Student Loan: $5,969
Undergraduate Enrollment - Fall 2001: 4,011
Average Class Size: 20
Demographics of Student Body: African-American 33%, Asian 14%, Caucasian 23%, Hispanic 25%
Percent of Students with Transfer-in Credit: 1%
Special Adult Programs: Yes

HOW DOES IT COMPARE?
College Experience:	★★★
Market Response:	★★★
Chance of Getting Out:	★★
Chance of Getting In:	★★★★★
Career Development Potential:	★★★
Total Cost:	Average Tuition
	Shorter than Average Time to Graduation

MOST POPULAR AREAS OF STUDY
Major Clusters:	Analytical/Computational, Applied Quantitative
Most Popular Majors:	Computer Information Systems 50%, Engineering Technologies 25%, Electronics & Computer Tech. 25%

UNIQUE FEATURES

— To help meet the needs of students who work or have other full-time responsibilities, DeVry offers accelerated Weekend Degree Programs. These programs, including Business Administration and Computer Information Systems at DeVry Chicago, condense the usual 15-week class term down to approximately 8 weeks, with all classes meeting on weekends.

—Technical Management and Information Technology degree-completion programs are also offered in an accelerated format.

Dominican University (Rosary College)

7900 West Division Street
River Forest, IL 60305
www.dom.edu, (708) 366-2490

COLLEGE PROFILE
Tuition 2002-2003: $16,620
Average Freshman Institutional Aid Award: $14,261
Percent of Students who Receive Freshman Institutional Aid Award: 96%
Average Student Loan: $3,051
Undergraduate Enrollment - Fall 2001: 1,189
Average Class Size: 14
Demographics of Student Body: African-American 5%, Asian 2%, Caucasian 73%, Hispanic 14%
Percent of Students with Transfer-in Credit: 40%
Special Adult Programs: Yes

HOW DOES IT COMPARE?
College Experience: ★★
Market Response: ★★★★
Chance of Getting Out: ★★★★
Chance of Getting In: ★★
Career Development Potential: ★★
Total Cost: High Tuition
Shorter than Average Time to Graduation

MOST POPULAR AREAS OF STUDY
Major Clusters: Analytical/Computational, Social Sciences
Most Popular Majors: Business Management 25%, Social Science 18%, Psychology 8%

UNIQUE FEATURES
— Accelerated Bachelor's and Master's Programs available in evening and weekend format.

— Small classes and a student-faculty ratio of 11 to 1.

Northeastern Illinois University
5500 N. Saint Louis Avenue
Chicago, IL 60625
www.neiu.edu, (773) 583-4050

COLLEGE PROFILE
Tuition 2002-2003: $3,330
Average Freshman Institutional Aid Award: $1,216
Percent of Students who Receive Freshman Institutional Aid Award: 5%
Average Student Loan: $2,365
Undergraduate Enrollment - Fall 2001: 8,324
Average Class Size: n/a
Demographics of Student Body: African-American 13%, Asian 14%, Caucasian 44%, Hispanic 27%
Percent of Students with Transfer-in Credit: 12%
Special Adult Programs: n/a

HOW DOES IT COMPARE?
College Experience: ★★★
Market Response: ★★★★
Chance of Getting Out: ★★★
Chance of Getting In: ★★★★★
Career Development Potential: ★★★
Total Cost: Low Tuition
Longer than Average Time to Graduation

MOST POPULAR AREAS OF STUDY
Major Clusters: Social Sciences, Verbal
Most Popular Majors: Education 25%, Liberal Arts 19%, Business Management 11%

UNIQUE FEATURES
Northeastern Illinois University's P.U.L.S.E. (Pre-University Laboratory School Endeavor) program nurtures middle school student's skills in reading, writing, math, social responsibility, leadership, technology, and cultural awareness.

Robert Morris College
401 South State Street
Chicago, IL 60605
www.rmcil.edu, (312) 935-6800

COLLEGE PROFILE
Tuition 2002-2003: $12,750
Average Freshman Institutional Aid Award: $2,114
Percent of Students who Receive Freshman Institutional Aid Award: 70%
Average Student Loan: $4,059
Undergraduate Enrollment - Fall 2001: 4,975
Average Class Size: 20
Demographics of Student Body: African-American 45%, Asian 3%, Caucasian 27%, Hispanic 25%
Percent of Students with Transfer-in Credit: 24%
Special Adult Programs: Yes

HOW DOES IT COMPARE?
College Experience: ★★★★★
Market Response: ★★★★★
Chance of Getting Out: ★★★★
Chance of Getting In: ★★★★★
Career Development Potential: ★★★★★
Total Cost: Average Tuition
                     Shorter than Average Time to Graduation

MOST POPULAR AREAS OF STUDY
Major Clusters: Analytical/Computational
Most Popular Majors: Business Management 97%,
                         Visual & Performing Arts 3%

UNIQUE FEATURES
— Concentrated, accelerated degree programs with lifetime job placement services.

— RMC awards more Associate Degrees (all disciplines combined) to minority graduates than any other institution in Illinois.

— Nationally, RMC is 16th-largest grantor of Bachelor Degrees in Business Administration to African-Americans.

Get In. Get Out. Get a Job. // 77

Saint Xavier University
3700 West 103rd Street
Chicago, IL 60655
www.sxu.edu, (773) 298-3000

COLLEGE PROFILE
Tuition 2002-2003: $15,750,
Average Freshman Institutional Aid Award: $5,087
Percent of Students who Receive Freshman Institutional Aid Award: 97%,
Average Student Loan: $3,665,
Undergraduate Enrollment - Fall 2001: 2,815
Average Class Size: 21
Demographics of Student Body: African-American 16%, Asian 2%, Caucasian 64%, Hispanic 12%
Percent of Students with Transfer-in Credit: 43%
Special Adult Programs: n/a

HOW DOES IT COMPARE?
College Experience: ★★★★
Market Response: ★★★
Chance of Getting Out: ★★
Chance of Getting In: ★★★★
Career Development Potential: ★★★★
Total Cost: High Tuition
Average Time to Graduation

MOST POPULAR AREAS OF STUDY
Major Clusters: Quantitative, Social Sciences
Most Popular Majors: Health Professions 20%, Education 18%, Business Management 16%

UNIQUE FEATURES
— "First generation" college students succeed at Saint Xavier; 73% of Saint Xavier Students will be the first in their family to graduate from college.

— Saint Xavier graduates are successful; 95% of Saint Xavier University graduates are employed in their major field of study or enrolled in graduate school within six months of graduation.

University of Illinois — Chicago
601 S. Morgan Street
Chicago, IL 60607
www.uic.edu, (312) 996-3000

COLLEGE PROFILE
Tuition 2002-2003: $4,944
Average Freshman Institutional Aid Award: $1,523
Percent of Students who Receive Freshman Institutional Aid Award: 37%
Average Student Loan: $2,931
Undergraduate Enrollment - Fall 2001: 16,140
Average Class Size: 33
Demographics of Student Body: African-American 10%, Asian 23%, Caucasian 45%, Hispanic 17%
Percent of Students with Transfer-in Credit: 59%
Special Adult Programs: n/a

HOW DOES IT COMPARE?
College Experience: ★★★
Market Response: ★★★
Chance of Getting Out: ★★★
Chance of Getting In: ★★★★★
Career Development Potential: ★★★★
Total Cost: Low Tuition
Longer than Average Time to Graduation

MOST POPULAR AREAS OF STUDY
Major Clusters: Analytical/Computational, Quantitative
Most Popular Majors: Business Management 21%, Psychology 11%
Engineering

UNIQUE FEATURES
— UIC's six health sciences colleges produce many of Illinois' doctors, nurses, and other health professionals.

— Incoming freshmen enrolled in the College of Liberal Arts and Sciences can take part in the Freshman Learning Cluster, a three-year pilot program developed to give students a more intimate and well-defined learning experience.

University of St. Francis
500 N. Wilcox Street
Joliet, IL 60435
www.stfrancis.edu, (815) 740-3360

COLLEGE PROFILE
Tuition 2002-2003: $16,030
Average Freshman Institutional Aid Award: $2,345
Percent of Students who Receive Freshman Institutional Aid Award: 69%
Average Student Loan: $1,657
Undergraduate Enrollment - Fall 2001: 2,858
Average Class Size: 20
Demographics of Student Body: African-American 4%, Asian 2%, Caucasian 81%, Hispanic 3%
Percent of Students with Transfer-in Credit: 58%
Special Adult Programs: Yes

HOW DOES IT COMPARE?
College Experience: ★★★
Market Response: ★
Chance of Getting Out: ★★
Chance of Getting In: ★★
Career Development Potential: ★★★★
Total Cost: High Tuition
Shorter than Average Time to Graduation

MOST POPULAR AREAS OF STUDY
Major Clusters: Verbal, Quantitative
Most Popular Majors: Multi/Interdisciplinary Studies 64%, Business Management 10%, Health Professions 8%

UNIQUE FEATURES
— Nursing students at USF who took the NCLEX-RN licensure examination during the time periods of April to September 2001 and October 2001 to March 2002 had a pass rate that exceeded the national average by 10 percent.

— USF is nationally-focused, with more than 100 locations in 19 states.

Butler University
4600 Sunset Avenue
Indianapolis, IN 46208
www.butler.edu, (800) 368-6852

COLLEGE PROFILE
Tuition 2002-2003: $19,990
Average Freshman Institutional Aid Award: $7,000
Percent of Students who Receive Freshman Institutional Aid Award: 84%
Average Student Loan: $3,488
Undergraduate Enrollment - Fall 2001: 3,483
Average Class Size: 20
Demographics of Student Body: African-American 4%, Asian 2%, Caucasian 91%, Hispanic 1%
Percent of Students with Transfer-in Credit: 10%
Special Adult Programs: n/a

HOW DOES IT COMPARE?
College Experience: ★★★
Market Response: ★★★★
Chance of Getting Out: ★★
Chance of Getting In: ★
Career Development Potential: ★★★★
Total Cost: High Tuition
                   Shorter than Average Time to Graduation

MOST POPULAR AREAS OF STUDY
Major Clusters: Analytical/Computational, Social Sciences
Most Popular Majors: Business Management 22%, Education 10%, Pharmacy Technology 9%

UNIQUE FEATURES
— Over 100 special interest student groups, including eight national sororities and eight national fraternities; music, dance and theatrical performance groups; a student newspaper, yearbook and literary magazine; academic clubs and honor societies; and a student-run television station.

— Cooperative Education Program allows students to integrate the strength of a business education with the skills and formal training of on the job experience by working and taking classes.

Franklin College of Indiana
501 East Monroe Street
Franklin, IN 46131
www.franklincoll.edu, (317) 738-8000

COLLEGE PROFILE
Tuition 2002-2003: $15,500
Average Freshman Institutional Aid Award: $4,202
Percent of Students who Receive Freshman Institutional Aid Award: 98%
Average Student Loan: $3,570
Undergraduate Enrollment - Fall 2001: 1,028
Average Class Size: 20
Demographics of Student Body: African-American 3%, Caucasian 94%, Hispanic 1%
Percent of Students with Transfer-in Credit: 30%
Special Adult Programs: n/a

HOW DOES IT COMPARE?
College Experience: ★★
Market Response: ★★★
Chance of Getting Out: ★★★
Chance of Getting In: ★★
Career Development Potential: ★
Total Cost: High Tuition
                    Shorter than Average Time to Graduation

MOST POPULAR AREAS OF STUDY
Major Clusters: Verbal, Social Sciences
Most Popular Majors: Education 22%, Social Sciences 16%
                     Communications 15%

UNIQUE FEATURES
— The department of mathematics and computing has achieved regional and national recognition for its innovative programs in mathematics and computing. The department has been named one of the top 100 success stories in the integration of computer technology into the classroom by EDUCOM, a national educational computing organization.

— Franklin, a city of 15,000, is located 30 minutes south of downtown Indianapolis. Students regularly go to Indianapolis for its restaurants, museums, music, shopping, and professional sports.

Huntington College

2303 College Avenue
Huntington, IN 46750
www.huntington.edu, (219) 356-6000

COLLEGE PROFILE
Tuition 2002-2003: $15,520
Average Freshman Institutional Aid Award: $4,646
Percent of Students who Receive Freshman Institutional Aid Award: 79%
Average Student Loan: $3,324
Undergraduate Enrollment - Fall 2001: 879
Average Class Size: 20
Demographics of Student Body: Asian 1%, Caucasian 97%, Hispanic 1%
Percent of Students with Transfer-in Credit: 35%
Special Adult Programs: n/a

HOW DOES IT COMPARE?
College Experience: ★★
Market Response: ★★★
Chance of Getting Out: ★★★
Chance of Getting In: ★★
Career Development Potential: ★★
Total Cost: High Tuition
                Shorter than Average Time to Graduation

MOST POPULAR AREAS OF STUDY
Major Clusters: Analytical/Computational, Social Sciences
Most Popular Majors: Education 18%, Religious Studies 12%
                           Business 10%

UNIQUE FEATURES
— Huntington College will offer a new program in special education next fall. The Indiana Professional Standards Board approved a proposed special education program by Huntington College, effective immediately. The special education program will lead students to a license for Exceptional Needs: Mild Intervention in grades K-6.

— Students in the EXCEL Program graduate with an accredited associate of science degree or a bachelor of science degree in organizational management, providing eligibility for graduate school. They also attend class one evening each week, thus minimizing interference with work schedules and family responsibilities.

Indiana Institute of Technology
1600 E. Washington Blvd.
Fort Wayne, IN 46803
www.indtech.edu, (219) 422-5561

COLLEGE PROFILE
Tuition 2002-2003: $14,848
Average Freshman Institutional Aid Award: $5,759
Percent of Students who Receive Freshman Institutional Aid Award: 96%
Average Student Loan: $4,700
Undergraduate Enrollment - Fall 2001: 2,757
Average Class Size: 22
Demographics of Student Body: African-American 15%, Caucasian 80%, Hispanic 1%
Percent of Students with Transfer-in Credit: 42%
Special Adult Programs: Yes

HOW DOES IT COMPARE?
College Experience: ★★★
Market Response: ★★★
Chance of Getting Out: ★★
Chance of Getting In: ★★★★
Career Development Potential: ★★★
Total Cost: High Tuition
                   Average Time to Graduation

MOST POPULAR AREAS OF STUDY
Major Clusters: Analytical/Computational, Applied Quantitative
Most Popular Majors: Business 85%, Engineering 15%

UNIQUE FEATURES
— Accelerated Degree Program provides the motivated student an alternative to traditional full-term course work. With an emphasis on intensive individual studies and with the aid of weekly classroom sessions, students progress at an advanced pace.

— Independent Study Program offers students the opportunity to complete their entire college degree without attending formal classes. Via mail, students are provided with the necessary course materials to guide them through the course work.

Marian College
3200 Cold Spring Road
Indianapolis, IN 46222
www.marian.edu, (317) 955-6000

COLLEGE PROFILE
Tuition 2002-2003: $16,000
Average Freshman Institutional Aid Award: $7,000
Percent of Students who Receive Freshman Institutional Aid Award: 95%
Average Student Loan: $3,100
Undergraduate Enrollment - Fall 2001: 1,261
Average Class Size: 17
Demographics of Student Body: African-American 16%, Asian 1%, Caucasian 79%, Hispanic 2%
Percent of Students with Transfer-in Credit: 12%
Special Adult Programs: Yes

HOW DOES IT COMPARE?
College Experience: ★★★
Market Response: ★
Chance of Getting Out: ★★
Chance of Getting In: ★★★★
Career Development Potential: ★★★
Total Cost: High Tuition
Shorter than Average Time to Graduation

MOST POPULAR AREAS OF STUDY
Major Clusters: Quantitative, Analytical/Computational
Most Popular Majors: Health Professions 22%, Business Management 19%, Education 16%

UNIQUE FEATURES
— Marian College offers many alternatives for adult students, including accelerated classes in Business and Management Information Systems, as well as late afternoon and evening classes for those students holding full-time jobs.

— Accelerated Program is a degree completion program in business based on a calendar of 5-week terms, 3 terms per semester, with courses offered at off-campus locations, as well as on campus.

University of Indianapolis
1400 E. Hanna Avenue
Indianapolis, IN 46227
www.uindy.edu, (317) 788-3368

COLLEGE PROFILE
Tuition 2002-2003: $15,820
Average Freshman Institutional Aid Award: $12,891
Percent of Students who Receive Freshman Institutional Aid Award: 75%
Average Student Loan: $2,803
Undergraduate Enrollment - Fall 2001: 2,843
Average Class Size: 17
Demographics of Student Body: African-American 8%, Asian 1%, Caucasian 76%, Hispanic 1%
Percent of Students with Transfer-in Credit: 20%
Special Adult Programs: Yes

HOW DOES IT COMPARE?
College Experience: ★★★
Market Response: ★★★
Chance of Getting Out: ★★
Chance of Getting In: ★★
Career Development Potential: ★★★★
Total Cost: High Tuition
Average Time to Graduation

MOST POPULAR AREAS OF STUDY
Major Clusters: Analytical/Computational, Social Sciences
Most Popular Majors: Business Management 20%, Education 18%, Psychology 10%

UNIQUE FEATURES
— The University of Indianapolis is in the southern suburbs of Indianapolis, just 10 minutes away from downtown with excellent opportunities for internships and volunteer experiences, as well as endless recreational, entertainment, and cultural events.

— The School for Adult Learning (SAL) is the full-service center for adult learners at the University of Indianapolis. Offering college-level credit courses for students pursuing associate degrees, bachelor's degrees, and certificate programs, SAL provides courses in convenient formats for working adults including traditional fifteen-week courses and accelerated courses.

Clarke College
1550 Clarke Drive
Dubuque, IA 52001
www.clarke.edu, (563) 588-6300

COLLEGE PROFILE
Tuition 2002-2003: $15,715
Average Freshman Institutional Aid Award: $6,690
Percent of Students who Receive Freshman Institutional Aid Award: 97%
Average Student Loan: $2,918
Undergraduate Enrollment - Fall 2001: 1,052
Average Class Size: 12
Demographics of Student Body: African-American 1%, Caucasian 93%, Hispanic 2%
Percent of Students with Transfer-in Credit: 54%
Special Adult Programs: Yes

HOW DOES IT COMPARE?
College Experience: ★★
Market Response: ★★★★
Chance of Getting Out: ★★★★
Chance of Getting In: ★★
Career Development Potential: ★★
Total Cost: High Tuition
Shorter than Average Time to Graduation

MOST POPULAR AREAS OF STUDY
Major Clusters: Quantitative, Analytical/Computational
Most Popular Majors: Health Professions 28%, Education 20%, Business Management 12%
Computer and Information Sciences 10%

UNIQUE FEATURES
— Time Saver Degree Programs are available for adults who have full-time jobs. Students can enroll full-time or part-time.

— Ninety-six percent of Clarke graduates are placed in jobs in their field of study or graduate school within six months of graduation.

Grand View College
1200 Grandview Avenue
Des Moines, IA 50316
www.gvc.edu, (515) 263-2800

COLLEGE PROFILE
Tuition 2002-2003: $14,194
Average Freshman Institutional Aid Award: $4,544
Percent of Students who Receive Freshman Institutional Aid Award: 100%
Average Student Loan: $5,271
Undergraduate Enrollment - Fall 2001: 1,378
Average Class Size: 20
Demographics of Student Body: African-American 4%, Asian 2%, Caucasian 65%, Hispanic 2%
Percent of Students with Transfer-in Credit: 60%
Special Adult Programs: Yes

HOW DOES IT COMPARE?
College Experience:	★★★
Market Response:	★
Chance of Getting Out:	★★
Chance of Getting In:	★★★★
Career Development Potential:	★★★★
Total Cost:	High Tuition
	Average Time to Graduation

MOST POPULAR AREAS OF STUDY
Major Clusters:	Quantitative, Analytical/Computational
Most Popular Majors:	Health Professions 22%, Business Management 20% Education 14%

UNIQUE FEATURES
— The Des Moines Advantage: The school's location makes it unique. It's a small college in the heart of Iowa's largest city, and it has have partnerships in Des Moines that are fantastic for students. GVC internships and practicums will pay dividends when students begin their career.

— At Grand View, students will spend four years working with faculty who care about them and are committed to providing the best education possible. They will give students support as well as inspiration.

Sullivan University
3101 Bardstown Road
Louisville, KY 40205
www.sullivan.edu, 502-456-6505

COLLEGE PROFILE
Tuition 2002-2003: $11,280
Average Freshman Institutional Aid Award: n/a
Percent of Students who Receive Freshman Institutional Aid Award: n/a
Average Student Loan: n/a
Undergraduate Enrollment - Fall 2001: 4,245
Average Class Size: 20
Demographics of Student Body: African American 17%, Caucasian 80%, Hispanic 2%, Native American 1%
Percent of Students with Transfer-in Credit: 8%
Special Adult Programs: Yes

HOW DOES IT COMPARE?
College Experience: ★★★
Market Response: ★★
Chance of Getting Out: ★★★
Chance of Getting In: ★★★★
Career Development Potential: ★★★★★
Total Cost: Average Tuition
Shorter than Average Time to Graduation

MOST POPULAR AREAS OF STUDY
Major Clusters: Analytical/Computational, Social Sciences
Most Popular Majors: Accounting, Business Administration, Culinary

UNIQUE FEATURES
Job-readiness is the key. At Sullivan University, you only take the classes you'll need to best perform in your chosen field. In most majors, Sullivan students concentrate exclusively in areas of career education during a 9-12 month Certificate or Diploma program. Then, if a student decides to continue toward the Associate or Bachelor's Degree, advanced and general education courses are taken during the final few months or quarters of each degree program, just the opposite of many college and university programs.

Dillard University

2601 Gentilly Boulevard
New Orleans, LA 70122
www.dillard.edu, (800) 216-6637

COLLEGE PROFILE

Tuition 2002-2003: $10,095
Average Freshman Institutional Aid Award: $2,500
Percent of Students who Receive Freshman Institutional Aid Award: 99%
Average Student Loan: $14,000
Undergraduate Enrollment - Fall 2001: 2,137
Average Class Size: 18
Demographics of Student Body: African-American 99%
Percent of Students with Transfer-in Credit: 20%
Special Adult Programs: n/a

HOW DOES IT COMPARE?

College Experience: ★★★
Market Response: ★★
Chance of Getting Out: ★★★
Chance of Getting In: ★★★★★
Career Development Potential: ★★
Total Cost: Average Tuition
                    Longer than Average Time to Graduation

MOST POPULAR AREAS OF STUDY

Major Clusters: Quantitative, Analytical/Computational
Most Popular Majors: Health Professions 34%, Business Management 13%
                        Physical Sciences 8%

UNIQUE FEATURES

The Office of Life Long Learning comprises evening, weekend and summer course offerings toward completion of the baccalaureate degree in seven major programs of study. The Office of Life Long Learning is designed to serve non-traditional students, as well as regular day students who need courses that are scheduled in the evening, weekend and summer.

Loyola University — New Orleans City College

6363 Saint Charles Avenue
New Orleans, LA 70118
www.loyno.edu, (504) 865-2011

COLLEGE PROFILE
Tuition 2002-2003: $18,700
Average Freshman Institutional Aid Award: $8,304
Percent of Students who Receive Freshman Institutional Aid Award: 92%
Average Student Loan: $3,017
Undergraduate Enrollment - Fall 2001: 3,688
Average Class Size: 20
Demographics of Student Body: African-American 27%, Asian 2%, Caucasian 60%, Hispanic 5%, Native American 1%
Percent of Students with Transfer-in Credit: 95%
Special Adult Programs: Yes

HOW DOES IT COMPARE?
College Experience: ★★★★★
Market Response: ★★★★
Chance of Getting Out: ★★
Chance of Getting In: ★★★
Career Development Potential: ★★★
Total Cost: High Tuition
Average Time to Graduation

MOST POPULAR AREAS OF STUDY
Major Clusters: Analytical/Computational, Verbal
Most Popular Majors: Health Professions 37%, Criminal Justice 20%, Computer & Information Sciences 11%

UNIQUE FEATURES
— Criminal Justice Degree programs (bachelor's and master's) are offered, both with nontraditional course scheduling.

— City College welcomes all adults interested in beginning or completing their degree and encourages them to call the City College office to arrange for a pre-admission conference. Recognizing that the adult student brings to education a diverse and varied experience, City College faculty work closely with each student to develop a critical stance and humanistic interpretation of the experience.

Xavier University of Louisiana
7325 Palmetto Street
New Orleans, LA 70125
www.xula.edu, (504) 486-7411

COLLEGE PROFILE
Tuition 2002-2003: $10,100
Average Freshman Institutional Aid Award: $5,068
Percent of Students who Receive Freshman Institutional Aid Award: 32%
Average Student Loan: $6,186
Undergraduate Enrollment - Fall 2001: 3,027
Average Class Size: 30
Demographics of Student Body: African-American 93%, Asian 2%, Caucasian 2%
Percent of Students with Transfer-in Credit: 5%
Special Adult Programs: Yes

HOW DOES IT COMPARE?
College Experience: ★★★
Market Response: ★★★
Chance of Getting Out: ★★
Chance of Getting In: ★★★
Career Development Potential: ★★
Total Cost: Average Tuition
Average Time to Graduation

MOST POPULAR AREAS OF STUDY
Major Clusters: Quantitative
Most Popular Majors: Natural Sciences/Math 56%, Social Sciences 13%
Humanities 8%

UNIQUE FEATURES
— Xavier ranks first in the nation in placing African-American students into medical schools, where it has been ranked for the last ten years. The 77% acceptance rate of Xavier graduates by medical schools is almost twice the national average, and 92% of those who enter medical schools complete their degree programs.

— Xavier ranks first in the nation in the number of African-American undergraduates receiving degrees in biology and the life sciences, as well as first in the nation in the number of African-American undergraduates receiving degrees in the physical sciences.

University of Southern Maine
96 Falmouth Street
Portland, ME 04103
www.usm.maine.edu, (207) 780-4141

COLLEGE PROFILE
Tuition 2002-2003: $4,537
Average Freshman Institutional Aid Award: $2,375
Percent of Students who Receive Freshman Institutional Aid Award: 19%
Average Student Loan: $2,851
Undergraduate Enrollment - Fall 2001: 8,726
Average Class Size: 20
Demographics of Student Body: African-American 1%, Asian 1%, Caucasian 97%, Native American 1%
Percent of Students with Transfer-in Credit: 40%
Special Adult Programs: Yes

HOW DOES IT COMPARE?
College Experience: ★★★
Market Response: ★★★
Chance of Getting Out: ★★★
Chance of Getting In: ★★★
Career Development Potential: ★★★
Total Cost: Low Tuition
Longer than Average Time to Graduation

MOST POPULAR AREAS OF STUDY
Major Clusters: Analytical/Computational, Social Sciences
Most Popular Majors: Social Sciences 23%, Business Management 13%, Health Professions 11%

UNIQUE FEATURES
— The residential campuses of Gorham and Portland are eight miles apart and located less than two hours from Boston. The Lewiston-Auburn campus, located in Lewiston, is 35 miles north of Portland.

— At the University of Southern Maine, you will find a small college atmosphere combined with the choices of a major university.

Get In. Get Out. Get a Job. // 93

College of Notre Dame of Maryland
4701 N. Charles Street
Baltimore, MD 21210
www.ndm.edu, (410) 435-0100

COLLEGE PROFILE
Tuition 2002-2003: $17,600
Average Freshman Institutional Aid Award: $8,186
Percent of Students who Receive Freshman Institutional Aid Award: 86%
Average Student Loan: $4,750
Undergraduate Enrollment - Fall 2001: 1,930
Average Class Size: 12
Demographics of Student Body: African-American 21%, Asian 2%,
    Caucasian 73%, Hispanic 2%
Percent of Students with Transfer-in Credit: 52%
Special Adult Programs: Yes

HOW DOES IT COMPARE?
College Experience:	★★★
Market Response:	★★
Chance of Getting Out:	★★★★
Chance of Getting In:	★★
Career Development Potential:	★★★★
Total Cost:	High Tuition
	Shorter than Average Time to Graduation

MOST POPULAR AREAS OF STUDY
Major Clusters:	Analytical/Computational, Social Sciences
Most Popular Majors:	Business Management 20%, Liberal Arts 13%
	Health Professions 10%

UNIQUE FEATURES
— Weekend College is a part-time undergraduate program for women and men, offering 11 majors. Courses are only on the weekends, scheduled so that students have time for work, family and personal lives. Students enjoy interacting with faculty as well as dedicated peers.

— Certificate Programs are also available.

University of Baltimore
1420 North St. Charles Street
Baltimore, MD 21210
www.ubalt.edu, (410) 837-4793

COLLEGE PROFILE
Tuition 2002-2003: $4,820
Average Freshman Institutional Aid Award: n/a
Percent of Students who Receive Freshman Institutional Aid Award: n/a
Average Student Loan: n/a
Undergraduate Enrollment - Fall 2001: 1,993
Average Class Size: 16
Demographics of Student Body: African-American 26%, Asian 3%, Caucasian 55%, Hispanic 2%
Percent of Students with Transfer-in Credit: 100%
Special Adult Programs: Yes

HOW DOES IT COMPARE?
College Experience: ★★★
Market Response: ★★★
Chance of Getting Out: ★★
Chance of Getting In: ★★★★
Career Development Potential: ★★★★★
Total Cost: Low Tuition
                    Average Time to Graduation

MOST POPULAR AREAS OF STUDY
Major Clusters: Analytical/Computational
Most Popular Majors: Business Management 45%, Protective Services 10%
                        Computer & Information Sciences 7%

UNIQUE FEATURES
— University of Baltimore, proud to be one of 13 schools under the umbrella of the University System of Maryland, boasts an appeal all its own. Offering the best of both worlds, UB's size promotes a feeling of intimacy while its three schools—Yale Gordon College of Liberal Arts, Merrick School of Business and the School of Law—deliver comprehensive programs.

— Web MBA Program is now offered.

University of Maryland — Baltimore County
1000 Hilltop Circle
Baltimore, MD 21250
www.umbc.edu, (410) 455-1000

COLLEGE PROFILE
Tuition 2002-2003: $5,910
Average Freshman Institutional Aid Award: $4,463
Percent of Students who Receive Freshman Institutional Aid Award: 34%
Average Student Loan: $4,914
Undergraduate Enrollment - Fall 2001: 9,101
Average Class Size: n/a
Demographics of Student Body: African-American 16%, Asian 18%, Caucasian 58%, Hispanic 3%
Percent of Students with Transfer-in Credit: 12%
Special Adult Programs: Yes

HOW DOES IT COMPARE?
College Experience: ★★★★
Market Response: ★★★★★
Chance of Getting Out: ★★★★
Chance of Getting In: ★★★★
Career Development Potential: ★★★★
Total Cost: Low Tuition
              Average Time to Graduation

MOST POPULAR AREAS OF STUDY
Major Clusters: Applied Quantitative, Social Sciences
Most Popular Majors: Computer and Information Sciences 29%, Social Sciences 15%

UNIQUE FEATURES
— Consistently ranked among the top five research universities nationally in production of bachelor's degrees in Information Technology.

— The Center for Women and Information Technology seeks to address and rectify the problem of women's under-represented as developers of IT and to enhance the understanding of the relationship between gender and IT.

Boston Architectural Center
320 Newbury Street
Boston, MA 02115
www.the-bac.edu, (617) 262-5000

COLLEGE PROFILE
Tuition 2002-2003: $7,438
Average Freshman Institutional Aid Award: $0
Percent of Students who Receive Freshman Institutional Aid Award: 0%
Average Student Loan: $4,360
Undergraduate Enrollment - Fall 2001: 358
Average Class Size: 20
Demographics of Student Body: African-American 3%, Asian 4%, Caucasian 65%, Hispanic 6%
Percent of Students with Transfer-in Credit: 16%
Special Adult Programs: Yes

HOW DOES IT COMPARE?
College Experience: ★★
Market Response: ★★★
Chance of Getting Out: ★★
Chance of Getting In: ★★★★
Career Development Potential: ★★★★
Total Cost: Low Tuition
                     Average Time to Graduation

MOST POPULAR AREAS OF STUDY
Major Clusters: Applied Quantitative
Most Popular Majors: Architecture 100%

UNIQUE FEATURES
— The BAC offers bachelor's and master's programs in architecture and interior design. Students have the unique opportunity to learn concurrently in academic and practice settings. Most course offerings take place in the evening so students can work in design firms during the day.

— The BAC's Continuing Education program offers courses and certificate programs to help architects and interior designers fulfill professional requirements. There is a variety of options for anyone seeking a design education.

College of Our Lady of the Elms
291 Springfield Street
Chicopee, MA 01013
www.elms.edu, (413) 594-2761

COLLEGE PROFILE
Tuition 2002-2003: $15,600
Average Freshman Institutional Aid Award: $5,115
Percent of Students who Receive Freshman Institutional Aid Award: 85%
Average Student Loan: $4,046
Undergraduate Enrollment - Fall 2001: 641
Average Class Size: 20
Demographics of Student Body: African-American 4%, Asian 1%, Caucasian 87%, Hispanic 4%
Percent of Students with Transfer-in Credit: 95%
Special Adult Programs: Yes

HOW DOES IT COMPARE?
College Experience: ★★★
Market Response: ★★
Chance of Getting Out: ★★★★
Chance of Getting In: ★★
Career Development Potential: ★★★
Total Cost: High Tuition
                 Shorter than Average Time to Graduation

MOST POPULAR AREAS OF STUDY
Major Clusters: Quantitative, Analytical/Computational
Most Popular Majors: Health Professions 24%, Business Management 12%
                      Public Administration 12%

UNIQUE FEATURES
In a recent survey of alumnae/i living in Western Massachusetts, more than 75% of respondents indicated that they are working in Human Services Professions—education, nursing, social work, ministry, and many others. Graduates are using their education to serve the people of the community, wherever they live, but especially in the Elms local community.

Eastern Nazarene College

23 East Elm Avenue
Quincy, MA 02170
www.enc.edu, (617) 745-3000

COLLEGE PROFILE
Tuition 2002-2003: $14,850
Average Freshman Institutional Aid Award: $6,588
Percent of Students who Receive Freshman Institutional Aid Award: 97%
Average Student Loan: $2,422
Undergraduate Enrollment - Fall 2001: 1,117
Average Class Size: 20
Demographics of Student Body: African-American 9%, Asian 2%, Caucasian 81%, Hispanic 3%
Percent of Students with Transfer-in Credit: 50%
Special Adult Programs: Yes

HOW DOES IT COMPARE?
College Experience: ★★★
Market Response: ★★★
Chance of Getting Out: ★★★
Chance of Getting In: ★★★★
Career Development Potential: ★★★
Total Cost: High Tuition
Average Time to Graduation

MOST POPULAR AREAS OF STUDY
Major Clusters: Analytical/Computational, Social Science
Most Popular Majors: Business Management 62%, Education 4%, Communications 4%

UNIQUE FEATURES
The Leadership Education for Adults (LEAD) Program was developed out of the desire to serve the adult population in Eastern Massachusetts, in a spirit open to innovation. Eastern Nazarene College seeks to understand the special requirements of adults who are interested in receiving a college degree, but must also continue meeting their professional and personal commitments. By combining theory and practical experience, the LEAD Program is designed for working adults.

Lesley University

29 Everett Street
Cambridge, MA 02138
www.lesley.edu, (617) 349-8300

COLLEGE PROFILE
Tuition 2002-2003: $18,300
Average Freshman Institutional Aid Award: $10,128
Percent of Students who Receive Freshman Institutional Aid Award: 76%
Average Student Loan: $4,681
Undergraduate Enrollment - Fall 2001: 2,277
Average Class Size: n/a
Demographics of Student Body: African-American 9%, Asian 5%, Caucasian 64%, Hispanic 7%
Percent of Students with Transfer-in Credit: 27%
Special Adult Programs: n/a

HOW DOES IT COMPARE?
College Experience: ★★★
Market Response: ★★★★★
Chance of Getting Out: ★★★
Chance of Getting In: ★★
Career Development Potential: ★★★★★
Total Cost: High Tuition
Shorter than Average Time to Graduation

MOST POPULAR AREAS OF STUDY
Major Clusters: Verbal, Social Sciences
Most Popular Majors: Education 55%, Liberal/General Studies 27%

UNIQUE FEATURES
— A multi-site university specializing in education, the arts, human services, and management. Lesley's six schools offer undergraduate and graduate programs at campuses in Cambridge and Boston, online and in 18 states.

— "The Lesley Dividend" is an opportunity to earn a free year of graduate study at Lesley.

Simmons College
300 The Fenway
Boston, MA 02115
www.simmons.edu, (617) 521-2000

COLLEGE PROFILE
Tuition 2002-2003: $21,680
Average Freshman Institutional Aid Award: $10,350
Percent of Students who Receive Freshman Institutional Aid Award: 71%
Average Student Loan: $3,538
Undergraduate Enrollment - Fall 2001: 1,186
Average Class Size: 20
Demographics of Student Body: African-American 7%, Asian 6%,
    Caucasian 72%, Hispanic 3%
Percent of Students with Transfer-in Credit: 14%
Special Adult Programs: Yes

HOW DOES IT COMPARE?
College Experience: ★★★★
Market Response: ★★★
Chance of Getting Out: ★★
Chance of Getting In: ★
Career Development Potential: ★★
Total Cost: High Tuition
                     Shorter than Average Time to Graduation

MOST POPULAR AREAS OF STUDY
Major Clusters: Quantitative, Social Sciences
Most Popular Majors: Health Professions 20%, Social Sciences 17%,
                         Psychology 9%

UNIQUE FEATURES
— Simmons is especially known for graduating students who have a sound liberal arts base and are exceptionally well-prepared for the world of work.

— Offerings include a nationally ranked undergraduate women's college, the world's only graduate business school designed specifically for women; highly respected coeducational graduate schools of library and information science, health studies, and social work; and graduate programs in education, communications management, and the liberal arts.

Suffolk University

8 Ashburton Place Beacon Hill
Boston, MA 02108
www.suffolk.edu, (617) 573-8000

COLLEGE PROFILE

Tuition 2002-2003: $17,610
Average Freshman Institutional Aid Award: $4,929
Percent of Students who Receive Freshman Institutional Aid Award: 76%
Average Student Loan: $3,721
Undergraduate Enrollment - Fall 2001: 3,532
Average Class Size: 20
Demographics of Student Body: African-American 4%, Asian 6%,
    Caucasian 58%, Hispanic 5%
Percent of Students with Transfer-in Credit: 25%
Special Adult Programs: Yes

HOW DOES IT COMPARE?

College Experience: ★★★★
Market Response: ★★★★
Chance of Getting Out: ★★
Chance of Getting In: ★★
Career Development Potential: ★★★
Total Cost: High Tuition
                      Average Time to Graduation

MOST POPULAR AREAS OF STUDY

Major Clusters: Analytical/Computational, Social Sciences
Most Popular Majors: Business Management 41%, Social Sciences 18%,
                      Communications 11%

UNIQUE FEATURES

— Suffolk University is a comprehensive private university located on Boston's historic Beacon Hill. This global university offers a wide range of undergraduate and graduate degrees in over 70 areas of study.

— Suffolk has three international campuses and over 20 Study Abroad agreements which allows students to graduate as citizens of the world.

University of Massachusetts — Boston

100 Morrissey Blvd.
Boston, MA 02125
www.umb.edu, (617) 287-6000

COLLEGE PROFILE
Tuition 2002-2003: $5,222
Average Freshman Institutional Aid Award: $1,722
Percent of Students who Receive Freshman Institutional Aid Award: 10%
Average Student Loan: $2,482
Undergraduate Enrollment - Fall 2001: 10,565
Average Class Size: 19
Demographics of Student Body: African-American 15%, Asian 12%, Caucasian 57%, Hispanic 7%
Percent of Students with Transfer-in Credit: 69%
Special Adult Programs: Yes

HOW DOES IT COMPARE?
College Experience: ★★★★
Market Response: ★★★★
Chance of Getting Out: ★★★
Chance of Getting In: ★★★
Career Development Potential: ★★★
Total Cost: Low Tuition
Longer than Average Time to Graduation

MOST POPULAR AREAS OF STUDY
Major Clusters: Social Sciences, Analytical/Computational
Most Popular Majors: Business Management 21%, Social Sciences 17%, Psychology 13%

UNIQUE FEATURES

— UMB's Distance Learning programs are rapidly expanding in response to increasing demand and technological innovation. Programs fall into two categories: (1) Online, web-based course; and (2) Classroom courses delivered to remote sites via video conferencing technology.

— UMass Boston brings the resources of a major university to people from all walks of life, offering undergraduate and graduate programs in approximately 90 fields of study, as well as advanced certificate programs through its Division of Corporate, Continuing and Distance Education.

Wentworth Institute of Technology

550 Huntington Avenue
Boston, MA 02115
www.wit.edu, (617) 989-4590

COLLEGE PROFILE
Tuition 2002-2003: $14,300
Average Freshman Institutional Aid Award: $422
Percent of Students who Receive Freshman Institutional Aid Award: 52%
Average Student Loan: $1,946
Undergraduate Enrollment - Fall 2001: 3,187
Average Class Size: n/a
Demographics of Student Body: African-American 6%, Asian 6%, Caucasian 66%, Hispanic 4%
Percent of Students with Transfer-in Credit: 15%
Special Adult Programs: Yes

HOW DOES IT COMPARE?
College Experience: ★★★
Market Response: ★★★
Chance of Getting Out: ★★
Chance of Getting In: ★★★★
Career Development Potential: ★★★
Total Cost: High Tuition
Average Time to Graduation

MOST POPULAR AREAS OF STUDY
Major Clusters: Applied Quantitative
Most Popular Majors: Engineering Technology 53%
Construction Trades 10%,
Computer and Information Sciences 23%

UNIQUE FEATURES

— Wentworth students acquire an understanding of basic scientific principles and become familiar with techniques, instruments, and equipment pertinent to their technology. Through laboratory work and practice, they apply their knowledge and skills to problems of technology. For this purpose, curricula are balanced between theory and practice.

— Wentworth offers high value in technology-based, career-oriented, affordable higher education on a small, supportive campus in the heart of a major urban center.

Calvin College

3201 Burton SE
Grand Rapids, MI 49546
www.calvin.edu, (616) 957-6000

COLLEGE PROFILE

Tuition 2002-2003: $15,750
Average Freshman Institutional Aid Award: $4,770
Percent of Students who Receive Freshman Institutional Aid Award: 93%
Average Student Loan: $4,000
Undergraduate Enrollment - Fall 2001: 4,221
Average Class Size: n/a
Demographics of Student Body: African-American 1%, Asian 2%, Caucasian 86%, Hispanic 1%
Percent of Students with Transfer-in Credit: 10%
Special Adult Programs: Yes

HOW DOES IT COMPARE?

College Experience: ★★★★
Market Response: ★★★★
Chance of Getting Out: ★★★★
Chance of Getting In: ★★★★
Career Development Potential: ★★★
Total Cost: High Tuition
Shorter than Average Time to Graduation

MOST POPULAR AREAS OF STUDY

Major Clusters: Analytical/Computational, Social Sciences
Most Popular Majors: Business Management 13%, Social Sciences 10% Education 9%,

UNIQUE FEATURES

— The Calvin Academy for Lifelong Learning (CALL) is a program for retired people at least 50 years of age.

— For almost forty years, Calvin College has challenged its best students with a campus-wide Honors Program—part of the school's overall mission to encourage academic excellence in a Christ-centered environment.

Madonna University

36600 Schoolcraft Road
Livonia, MI 48150
www.munet.edu, (734) 432-5300

COLLEGE PROFILE
Tuition 2002-2003: $8,350
Average Freshman Institutional Aid Award: $6,067
Percent of Students who Receive Freshman Institutional Aid Award: 60%
Average Student Loan: $3,329
Undergraduate Enrollment - Fall 2001: 3,078
Average Class Size: 17
Demographics of Student Body: African-American 11%, Asian 1%, Caucasian 77%, Hispanic 3%, Native American 1%
Percent of Students with Transfer-in Credit: 64%
Special Adult Programs: Yes

HOW DOES IT COMPARE?
College Experience: ★★★
Market Response: ★★★
Chance of Getting Out: ★★★
Chance of Getting In: ★★
Career Development Potential: ★★★★
Total Cost: Average Tuition
                     Shorter than Average Time to Graduation

MOST POPULAR AREAS OF STUDY
Major Clusters: Quantitative, Analytical/Computational
Most Popular Majors: Health Professions 16%, Business Management 14%, Education 14%

UNIQUE FEATURES
— The E2College offers a range of online courses and programs for working adults and students at a distance from the University.

— Weekend Pathways provides maximum flexibility for degree completion by combining weekend classes with online courses, telecourses, and credit for prior learning.

Wayne State University
656 W. Kirby
Detroit, MI 48202
www.wayne.edu, (313) 577-2424

COLLEGE PROFILE
Tuition 2002-2003: $4,330
Average Freshman Institutional Aid Award: $2,935
Percent of Students who Receive Freshman Institutional Aid Award: 26%
Average Student Loan: $2,593
Undergraduate Enrollment - Fall 2001: 18,093
Average Class Size: 20
Demographics of Student Body: African-American 30%, Asian 5%, Caucasian 50%, Hispanic 2%
Percent of Students with Transfer-in Credit: 34%
Special Adult Programs: Yes

HOW DOES IT COMPARE?
College Experience: ★★★
Market Response: ★★★
Chance of Getting Out: ★★
Chance of Getting In: ★★★
Career Development Potential: ★★★★
Total Cost: Low Tuition
                 Average Time to Graduation

MOST POPULAR AREAS OF STUDY
Major Clusters: Analytical/Computational, Social Sciences
Most Popular Majors: Business Management 16%, Education 13%, Health Professions 12%

UNIQUE FEATURES
— More than 60 percent of the practicing physicians in southeastern Michigan received all or part of their training at the School of Medicine.

— Recent investments of more than $300 million in facilities, including a new building for the College of Pharmacy and Allied Health Professions, a Law School expansion, a Fitness Center, and a new Welcome Center.

Augsburg College
2211 Riverside Avenue
Minneapolis, MN 55454
www.augsburg.edu, (612) 330-1000

COLLEGE PROFILE
Tuition 2002-2003: $18,193
Average Freshman Institutional Aid Award: $6,106
Percent of Students who Receive Freshman Institutional Aid Award: 85%
Average Student Loan: $5,140
Undergraduate Enrollment - Fall 2001: 2,780
Average Class Size: 16
Demographics of Student Body: African-American 5%, Asian 3%, Caucasian 69%, Hispanic 1%, Native American 1%
Percent of Students with Transfer-in Credit: 61%
Special Adult Programs: Yes

HOW DOES IT COMPARE?
College Experience: ★★★
Market Response: ★★★
Chance of Getting Out: ★
Chance of Getting In: ★
Career Development Potential: ★★★★
Total Cost: High Tuition
                     Average Time to Graduation

MOST POPULAR AREAS OF STUDY
Major Clusters: Analytical/Computational, Social Sciences
Most Popular Majors: Business Management 29%, Education 17%, Social Sciences 10%

UNIQUE FEATURES
— Physician's Assistant Program provides students with the opportunity to graduate with a Master's Degree in Physician's Assistant Studies.

— The College's location also provides access for all of Augsburg's students to participate in community service and internship experiences that not only enhance their classroom learning but also prepare them for life's work in a multi-cultural society.

Concordia College — Moorhead

901 S. 8th Street
Moorhead, MN 56562
www.cord.edu, (218) 299-4000

COLLEGE PROFILE
Tuition 2002-2003: $15,635
Average Freshman Institutional Aid Award: n/a
Percent of Students who Receive Freshman Institutional Aid Award: n/a
Average Student Loan: $4,938
Undergraduate Enrollment - Fall 2001: 2,766
Average Class Size: 21
Demographics of Student Body: Caucasian 92%, International 5%, Asian 1%, Hispanic 1%
Percent of Students with Transfer-in Credit: 3%
Special Adult Programs: Yes

HOW DOES IT COMPARE?
College Experience: ★★★★
Market Response: ★★★★
Chance of Getting Out: ★★★★
Chance of Getting In: ★★
Career Development Potential: ★★
Total Cost: High Tuition
Shorter than Average Time to Graduation

MOST POPULAR AREAS OF STUDY
Major Clusters: Social Sciences, Analytical/Computational
Most Popular Majors: Education 23%, Business Management 15%
Biological Sciences 10%

UNIQUE FEATURES
— At Concordia College there are 13 computer labs equipped with more than 180 PC and Macintosh computers.

— ACCORD is a program that helps adult students take advantage of their experiences and background knowledge. In many cases, previous college-level study can be applied toward a degree.

Belhaven College
1500 Peachtree Street
Jackson, MS 39202
www.belhaven.edu, (601) 968-5930

COLLEGE PROFILE
Tuition 2002-2003: $11,580
Average Freshman Institutional Aid Award: $5,125
Percent of Students who Receive Freshman Institutional Aid Award: 100%
Average Student Loan: $3,658
Undergraduate Enrollment - Fall 2001: 1,666
Average Class Size: 20
Demographics of Student Body: African-American 34%, Asian 1%, Caucasian 62%, Hispanic 1%, Native American 1%
Percent of Students with Transfer-in Credit: 40%
Special Adult Programs: Yes

HOW DOES IT COMPARE?
College Experience: ★★★
Market Response: ★★★★
Chance of Getting Out: ★★
Chance of Getting In: ★★★
Career Development Potential: ★★★
Total Cost: Average Tuition
Shorter than Average Time to Graduation

MOST POPULAR AREAS OF STUDY
Major Clusters: Analytical/Computational, Social Sciences
Most Popular Majors: Business Management 42%, Education 11%, Psychology 11%

UNIQUE FEATURES
— Adult Aspire is an accelerated degree program through which one can earn a BBA, BSM, MBA or MSM degree. Classes meet one time per week and are offered at convenient locations near downtown Jackson.

— Belhaven College offers two non-traditional graduate education programs: The Master of Education which meets the needs of professional educators who desire a graduate speciality; and the Master of Arts in Teaching for students who hold a bachelor's degree and wish to teach but have not completed an undergraduate teacher education program.

Millsaps College
1701 North State Street
Jackson, MS 39210
www.millsaps.edu, (601) 974-1000

COLLEGE PROFILE
Tuition 2002-2003: $16,364
Average Freshman Institutional Aid Award: $12,127
Percent of Students who Receive Freshman Institutional Aid Award: 93%
Average Student Loan: $4,006
Undergraduate Enrollment - Fall 2001: 1,221
Average Class Size: 17
Demographics of Student Body: African-American 11%, Asian 3%, Caucasian 84%, Hispanic 1%
Percent of Students with Transfer-in Credit: 5%
Special Adult Programs: Yes

HOW DOES IT COMPARE?
College Experience: ★★★★
Market Response: ★★
Chance of Getting Out: ★★★
Chance of Getting In: ★★
Career Development Potential: ★★★
Total Cost: High Tuition
 Shorter than Average Time to Graduation

MOST POPULAR AREAS OF STUDY
Major Clusters: Analytical/Computational, Social Sciences
Most Popular Majors: Business Management 22%, Psychology 10%, English Language 9%

UNIQUE FEATURES
— The Adult Degree Program was established in 1982 to meet the needs of non-traditional students who wish to pursue a degree as full-time or part-time students. This program features individualized academic advising, a required seminar, evaluation of previous college work, credit for prior learning, and the opportunity for independent directed study.

— Renaissance MBA Program and Project of Research in the Yucatan.

Deaconess College of Nursing

6150 Oakland Avenue
Saint Louis, MO 63139
www.deaconess.edu, (314) 768-3044

COLLEGE PROFILE
Tuition 2002-2003: $9,800
Average Freshman Institutional Aid Award: $1,685
Percent of Students who Receive Freshman Institutional Aid Award: 59%
Average Student Loan: $4,066
Undergraduate Enrollment - Fall 2001: 229
Average Class Size: 30
Demographics of Student Body: African-American 23%, Asian 1%, Caucasian 73%, Hispanic 1%
Percent of Students with Transfer-in Credit: 10%
Special Adult Programs: Yes

HOW DOES IT COMPARE?
College Experience: ★★
Market Response: ★
Chance of Getting Out: ★★
Chance of Getting In: ★★★★
Career Development Potential: ★★★
Total Cost: Average Tuition
              Longer than Average Time to Graduation

MOST POPULAR AREAS OF STUDY
Major Clusters: Quantitative
Most Popular Majors: Health Professions 100%

UNIQUE FEATURES
DCN's Associate of Science in Nursing (ASN) Program offers a quick, convenient track for current licensed practical nurses (LPNs) who want to become RNs. The program was designed with today's working student in mind. Once program prerequisites are met, LPNs can achieve RN status in just three semesters. Students may join the program in either the fall or spring and may attend day, evening or weekend classes.

Harris-Stowe State College

3026 Laclede Avenue
Saint Louis, MO 63103
www.hssc.edu, (314) 340-3366

COLLEGE PROFILE
Tuition 2002-2003: $2,895
Average Freshman Institutional Aid Award: $961
Percent of Students who Receive Freshman Institutional Aid Award: 65%
Average Student Loan: $1,211
Undergraduate Enrollment - Fall 2001: 1,835
Average Class Size: 20
Demographics of Student Body: African-American 77%, Caucasian 19%, Hispanic 1%
Percent of Students with Transfer-in Credit: 50%
Special Adult Programs: Yes

HOW DOES IT COMPARE?
College Experience: ★★
Market Response: ★
Chance of Getting Out: ★★
Chance of Getting In: ★★★★★
Career Development Potential: ★★★★
Total Cost: Low Tuition
              Longer than Average Time to Graduation

MOST POPULAR AREAS OF STUDY
Major Clusters: Social Sciences, Analytical/Computational
Most Popular Majors: Education 57%, Business Management 31%
                      Protective Service 7%

UNIQUE FEATURES
Students who attend Harris-Stowe can expect many exciting changes in the next five years, including an unprecedented period of expansion on the HSSC campus and the widening of course and degree options. The future for the college is bright, and the school welcomes students who are looking for a high-quality, affordable education opportunity.

Lindenwood University
209 South Kings Highway
St. Charles, MO 63301
www.lindenwood.edu, (636) 949-2000

COLLEGE PROFILE
Tuition 2002-2003: $11,200
Average Freshman Institutional Aid Award: $5,659
Percent of Students who Receive Freshman Institutional Aid Award: 96%
Average Student Loan: $2,662
Undergraduate Enrollment - Fall 2001: 4,199
Average Class Size: 21
Demographics of Student Body: African-American 8%, Asian 1%,
    Caucasian 85%, Hispanic 1%, Native American 1%,
Percent of Students with Transfer-in Credit: 16%
Special Adult Programs: Yes

HOW DOES IT COMPARE?
College Experience: ★★
Market Response: ★★★★
Chance of Getting Out: ★★★
Chance of Getting In: ★★★★★
Career Development Potential: ★★
Total Cost: Average Tuition
Longer than Average Time to Graduation

MOST POPULAR AREAS OF STUDY
Major Clusters: Analytical/Computational, Social Sciences
Most Popular Majors: Business Management 44%, Education 14%, Communications 10%

UNIQUE FEATURES
— A $12 million campus center will become the focal point of the campus and the City of St. Charles. The campus center will be a hub of activity at Lindenwood, with an around-the-clock computer lab, a full-service food court, Career Development services and more.

— Accelerated Evening College program is offered. There are many different majors available through this program, including Business Administration, Human Resources Management, and General Studies.

Maryville University of Saint Louis
13550 Conway Road
Saint Louis, MO 63141
www.maryville.edu, (800) 627-9855

COLLEGE PROFILE
Tuition 2002-2003: $14,400
Average Freshman Institutional Aid Award: $6,026
Percent of Students who Receive Freshman Institutional Aid Award: 78%
Average Student Loan: $2,422
Undergraduate Enrollment - Fall 2001: 2,573
Average Class Size: 20
Demographics of Student Body: African-American 5%, Asian 1%, Caucasian 73%, Hispanic 1%
Percent of Students with Transfer-in Credit: 71%
Special Adult Programs: Yes

HOW DOES IT COMPARE?
College Experience: ★★★
Market Response: ★★
Chance of Getting Out: ★★★★
Chance of Getting In: ★★★
Career Development Potential: ★★★
Total Cost: High Tuition
Shorter than Average Time to Graduation

MOST POPULAR AREAS OF STUDY
Major Clusters: Analytical/Computational, Quantitative
Most Popular Majors: Business Management 39%, Health Professions 25% Psychology 12%

UNIQUE FEATURES
— Four new campus buildings since 1997: Anheuser-Busch Academic Center, Art & Design Building, University Auditorium and University Center.

— Adjacent to Maryville Corporate Centre and St. Luke's Medical Center providing convenient access to internships.

National American University
200 Blue Ridge Boulevard
Kansas City, MO 64133
www.national.edu, (816) 353-4554

COLLEGE PROFILE
Tuition 2002-2003: $9,600
Average Freshman Institutional Aid Award: $0
Percent of Students who Receive Freshman Institutional Aid Award: 0%
Average Student Loan: $3,295
Undergraduate Enrollment - Fall 2001: 342
Average Class Size: 14
Demographics of Student Body: African-American 21%, Asian 3%, Caucasian 73%, Hispanic 3%
Percent of Students with Transfer-in Credit: 78%
Special Adult Programs: Yes

HOW DOES IT COMPARE?
College Experience: ★★★
Market Response: ★★★★
Chance of Getting Out: ★★★★
Chance of Getting In: ★★★★
Career Development Potential: ★★
Total Cost: Average Tuition
Longer than Average Time to Graduation

MOST POPULAR AREAS OF STUDY
Major Clusters: Applied Quantitative, Analytical/Computational
Most Popular Majors: Computer/Information Sciences 52%, Business Management 48%

UNIQUE FEATURES
— The Microsoft curriculum and advanced Information Technology (IT) offerings, in combination with the Sylvan Prometric Testing Center have been the "hot spot" for the Kansas City campus. Degrees in business, accounting and applied management are prospering.

— Accelerated Adult programs available.

Rockhurst University
1100 Rockhurst Road
Kansas City, MO 64110
www.rockhurst.edu, (816) 501-4000

COLLEGE PROFILE
Tuition 2002-2003: $15,140
Average Freshman Institutional Aid Award: $6,115
Percent of Students who Receive Freshman Institutional Aid Award: 98%
Average Student Loan: $4,475
Undergraduate Enrollment - Fall 2001: 2,034
Average Class Size: 15
Demographics of Student Body: African-American 9%, Asian 3%,
     Caucasian 78%, Hispanic 4%, Native American 1%
Percent of Students with Transfer-in Credit: 61%
Special Adult Programs: Yes

HOW DOES IT COMPARE?
College Experience: ★★★★★
Market Response: ★★★★
Chance of Getting Out: ★★★★
Chance of Getting In: ★★
Career Development Potential: ★★★
Total Cost: High Tuition
                     Shorter than Average Time to Graduation

MOST POPULAR AREAS OF STUDY
Major Clusters: Analytical/Computational, Quantitative
Most Popular Majors: Business Management 30%, Health Professions 18%,
                         Social Sciences 12%

UNIQUE FEATURES
—One in ten alumni is president, chief executive officer, or owner of his or her own company or organization.

— The MBA program is the largest in the Kansas City metropolitan area. Kansas City-based companies that consistently send students to the program include Sprint, Hallmark, Yellow Freight, Farmland Industries, Cerner, DST Systems and Honeywell.

Southwest Missouri State University

901 South National
Springfield, MO 65804
www.smsu.edu, (417) 836-5000

COLLEGE PROFILE

Tuition 2002-2003: $3,748
Average Freshman Institutional Aid Award: $2,441
Percent of Students who Receive Freshman Institutional Aid Award: 63%
Average Student Loan: $2,954
Undergraduate Enrollment - Fall 2001: 14,699
Average Class Size: 20
Demographics of Student Body: African-American 3%, Asian 1%, Caucasian 88%, Hispanic 1%, Native American 1%
Percent of Students with Transfer-in Credit: 66%
Special Adult Programs: Yes

HOW DOES IT COMPARE?

College Experience: ★★★
Market Response: ★★★
Chance of Getting Out: ★★★
Chance of Getting In: ★★★★
Career Development Potential: ★★★
Total Cost: Low Tuition
Longer than Average Time to Graduation

MOST POPULAR AREAS OF STUDY

Major Clusters: Analytical/Computational, Social Sciences
Most Popular Majors: Business Management 33%, Education 15%, Communications 8%

UNIQUE FEATURES

— SMSU offers the opportunities and advantages of Missouri's second largest university.

— SMSU offers quality academic programs that focus on the career success of its students.

University of Missouri — Saint Louis

8001 Natural Bridge Road
Saint Louis, MO 63121
www.umsl.edu, (314) 516-5000

COLLEGE PROFILE
Tuition 2002-2003: $5,543
Average Freshman Institutional Aid Award: $6,753
Percent of Students who Receive Freshman Institutional Aid Award: 25%
Average Student Loan: $5,723
Undergraduate Enrollment - Fall 2001: 12,251
Average Class Size: 27
Demographics of Student Body: African-American 14%, Asian 3%, Caucasian 77%, Hispanic 1%
Percent of Students with Transfer-in Credit: 68%
Special Adult Programs: n/a

HOW DOES IT COMPARE?
College Experience: ★
Market Response: ★★
Chance of Getting Out: ★★
Chance of Getting In: ★★★★
Career Development Potential: ★★★★
Total Cost: Low Tuition
Average Time to Graduation

MOST POPULAR AREAS OF STUDY
Major Clusters: Analytical/Computational, Social Sciences
Most Popular Majors: Business Management 28%, Education 19%, Social Sciences 11%

UNIQUE FEATURES
— Accredited On-Line MBA program. Part-time Engineering Program.

— More than 400 St. Louis area companies and organizations offering internships, cooperative education programs, and work study program.

Montana State University — Billings
1500 N. 30th Street
Billings, MT 59101
www.msubillings.edu, (406) 657-2011

COLLEGE PROFILE
Tuition 2002-2003: $3,799
Average Freshman Institutional Aid Award: $5,287
Percent of Students who Receive Freshman Institutional Aid Award: 73%
Average Student Loan: $2,992
Undergraduate Enrollment - Fall 2001: 3,870
Average Class Size: 25
Demographics of Student Body: Asian 1%, Caucasian 84%, Hispanic 3%, Native American 7%
Percent of Students with Transfer-in Credit: 10%
Special Adult Programs: Yes

HOW DOES IT COMPARE?
College Experience: ★★★
Market Response: ★
Chance of Getting Out: ★★★
Chance of Getting In: ★★★★★
Career Development Potential: ★★★★
Total Cost: Low Tuition
                Longer than Average Time to Graduation

MOST POPULAR AREAS OF STUDY
Major Clusters: Analytical/Computational, Social Sciences
Most Popular Majors: Education 43%, Visual Arts 41%, Business Management 23%

UNIQUE FEATURES
— The University's 112-acre campus is located in Billings, Montana, which has a population of over 100,000 residents.

— The community of Billings is ideal to explore opportunities in tune with your professional goals through internships, cooperative education programs, practicum, and field experiences

Rocky Mountain College
1511 Poly Drive
Billings, MT 59102
www.rocky.edu, (406) 657-1000

COLLEGE PROFILE
Tuition 2002-2003: $18,445
Average Freshman Institutional Aid Award: $4,227
Percent of Students who Receive Freshman Institutional Aid Award: 100%
Average Student Loan: $3,601
Undergraduate Enrollment - Fall 2001: 784
Average Class Size: 16
Demographics of Student Body: African-American 1%, Asian 1%,
    Caucasian 87%, Hispanic 1%, Native American 8%
Percent of Students with Transfer-in Credit: 47%
Special Adult Programs: Yes

HOW DOES IT COMPARE?
College Experience: ★★★
Market Response: ★★
Chance of Getting Out: ★★
Chance of Getting In: ★★★★★
Career Development Potential: ★★★★
Total Cost: High Tuition
Longer than Average Time to Graduation

MOST POPULAR AREAS OF STUDY
Major Clusters: Analytical/Computational, Quantitative
Most Popular Majors: Business Management 24%, Education 16%, Health Professions 14%

UNIQUE FEATURES
Rocky provides the same academic level of education as universities that offer four-year bachelor degrees, but Rocky offers small classes—the average class size is 16. Student will get to know their classmates, and can easily make appointments with professors to ask further questions, get advice, or receive assistance.

Clarkson College
101 S. 42nd Street
Omaha, NE 68131
www.clarksoncollege.edu, (402) 552-3100

COLLEGE PROFILE
Tuition 2002-2003: $8,835
Average Freshman Institutional Aid Award: $2,984
Percent of Students who Receive Freshman Institutional Aid Award: 51%
Average Student Loan: $7,015
Undergraduate Enrollment - Fall 2001: 274
Average Class Size: n/a
Demographics of Student Body: African-American 5%, Caucasian 90%, Hispanic 3%
Percent of Students with Transfer-in Credit: 54%
Special Adult Programs: Yes

HOW DOES IT COMPARE?
College Experience: ★★
Market Response: ★★
Chance of Getting Out: ★★★★★
Chance of Getting In: ★★★
Career Development Potential: ★★★★★
Total Cost: Average Tuition
Shorter than Average Time to Graduation

MOST POPULAR AREAS OF STUDY
Major Clusters: Quantitative
Most Popular Majors: Health Professions 95%, Business Management 5%

UNIQUE FEATURES
Clarkson College will become a premier private health sciences college that educates and trains students and professionals to provide outstanding health care services to patients, families, employers, and the community.

College of St. Mary
1901 South 72nd Street
Omaha, NE 68124
www.csm.edu, (402) 399-2400

COLLEGE PROFILE
Tuition 2002-2003: $14,700
Average Freshman Institutional Aid Award: $5,119
Percent of Students who Receive Freshman Institutional Aid Award: 45%
Average Student Loan: $3,419
Undergraduate Enrollment - Fall 2001: 930
Average Class Size: 11
Demographics of Student Body: African-American 5%, Asian 1%, Caucasian 90%, Hispanic 3%, Native American 1%
Percent of Students with Transfer-in Credit: 40%
Special Adult Programs: Yes

HOW DOES IT COMPARE?
College Experience: ★★
Market Response: ★★
Chance of Getting Out: ★
Chance of Getting In: ★★
Career Development Potential: ★★★★
Total Cost: High Tuition
Shorter than Average Time to Graduation

MOST POPULAR AREAS OF STUDY
Major Clusters: Quantitative, Analytical/Computational
Most Popular Majors: Health Professions 16%, Business Management 14%, Education 14%

UNIQUE FEATURES
— Region's only residential campus to offer housing for single mothers and their children.

— Region's only 4-year paralegal studies program approved by the American Bar Association.

Creighton University

2500 California Plaza
Omaha, NE 68178
www.creighton.edu, (402) 280-2700

COLLEGE PROFILE
Tuition 2002-2003: $18,200
Average Freshman Institutional Aid Award: $7,072
Percent of Students who Receive Freshman Institutional Aid Award: 87%
Average Student Loan: $4,285
Undergraduate Enrollment - Fall 2001: 3,679
Average Class Size: 20
Demographics of Student Body: African-American 3%, Asian 10%, Caucasian 78%, Hispanic 4%, Native American 1%
Percent of Students with Transfer-in Credit: 38%
Special Adult Programs: Yes

HOW DOES IT COMPARE?
College Experience: ★★★★
Market Response: ★★★★
Chance of Getting Out: ★★★★
Chance of Getting In: ★★
Career Development Potential: ★★
Total Cost:　　　　High Tuition
　　　　　　　　　Shorter than Average Time to Graduation

MOST POPULAR AREAS OF STUDY
Major Clusters:　　　Quantitative, Analytical/Computational
Most Popular Majors:　Health Professions 27%, Business Management 19%, Biological Sciences 14%

UNIQUE FEATURES
— Creighton University is highly diverse academically, with three undergraduate and five professional schools.

— A large percentage of Creighton's undergraduates go on to professional school after graduation.

Morrison University
140 Washington Street
Reno, NV 89503
www.morrison.edu, (702) 323-4145

COLLEGE PROFILE
Tuition 2002-2003: $7,440
Average Freshman Institutional Aid Award: $0
Percent of Students who Receive Freshman Institutional Aid Award: 0%
Average Student Loan: $0
Undergraduate Enrollment - Fall 2001: 150
Average Class Size: 10
Demographics of Student Body: African-American 2%, Asian 5%, Caucasian 85%, Hispanic 5%, Native American 2%
Percent of Students with Transfer-in Credit: 55%
Special Adult Programs: Yes

HOW DOES IT COMPARE?
College Experience: ★★★
Market Response: ★
Chance of Getting Out: ★★★
Chance of Getting In: ★★★★
Career Development Potential: ★★★★★
Total Cost: Low Tuition
               Shorter than Average Time to Graduation

MOST POPULAR AREAS OF STUDY
Major Clusters: Analytical/Computational
Most Popular Majors: Business Management 100%

UNIQUE FEATURES
— Most Associate Degree programs are offered during the day or evening.

— The advanced courses associated with the Bachelor Degree are presently offered only in the evening. The MBA courses are offered on Friday evenings and on Saturday. This means students attend school with other students who are serious about a career, and benefit from the experience and maturity of other students.

— Students can earn an Associate Degree in a specialized area and, with additional study, earn the Bachelor of Science Degree. In many cases, students can mix and match their Associate and Bachelor Degree programs to fit their career goals.

University of Nevada — Las Vegas

4505 South Maryland Parkway
Las Vegas, NV 89154
www.unlv.edu, (702) 895-3011

COLLEGE PROFILE
Tuition 2002-2003: $2,490
Average Freshman Institutional Aid Award: $5,710
Percent of Students who Receive Freshman Institutional Aid Award: 77%
Average Student Loan: $3,210
Undergraduate Enrollment - Fall 2001: 17,250
Average Class Size: 29
Demographics of Student Body: African-American 7%, Asian 12%, Caucasian 58%, Hispanic 10%, Native American 1%
Percent of Students with Transfer-in Credit: 15%
Special Adult Programs: Yes

HOW DOES IT COMPARE?
College Experience: ★★
Market Response: ★★★★
Chance of Getting Out: ★★★
Chance of Getting In: ★★★★★
Career Development Potential: ★★
Total Cost: Low Tuition
Longer than Average Time to Graduation

MOST POPULAR AREAS OF STUDY
Major Clusters: Analytical/Computational, Social Sciences
Most Popular Majors: Business Management 31%, Education 17%, Health Professions 8%

UNIQUE FEATURES
— UNLV's development embraces the traditional values of higher education adapted for the global community of the 21st century. The University increasingly will concentrate its resources on programs that are student centered, demonstrably excellent, and responsive to the needs of the local and regional community.

— Students attend classes at an attractive 335-acre campus in metropolitan Las Vegas. Close by are new homes and apartments, schools, shopping centers, restaurants, and all the conveniences of a modern cosmopolitan area.

Southern New Hampshire University

2500 N. River Road
Manchester, NH 03106
www.snhu.edu, (603) 668-2211

COLLEGE PROFILE
Tuition 2002-2003: $16,536
Average Freshman Institutional Aid Award: $4,250
Percent of Students who Receive Freshman Institutional Aid Award: 80%
Average Student Loan: $5,140
Undergraduate Enrollment - Fall 2001: 3,907
Average Class Size: 25
Demographics of Student Body: African-American 2%, Asian 1%, Caucasian 50%
Percent of Students with Transfer-in Credit: 30%
Special Adult Programs: Yes

HOW DOES IT COMPARE?
College Experience: ★★★
Market Response: ★★★★
Chance of Getting Out: ★★
Chance of Getting In: ★★
Career Development Potential: ★★★★
Total Cost: High Tuition
Shorter than Average Time to Graduation

MOST POPULAR AREAS OF STUDY
Major Clusters: Analytical/Computational, Applied Quantitative
Most Popular Majors: Business Management 81%,
Computer/ Information Sciences- 7%
Parks, Recreation, Leisure and Fitness -3%

UNIQUE FEATURES
SNHU and Dell have teamed up to offer the benefit of participating in the Dell University Program. This is great news for students, since the Dell University Program offers award-winning technology, flexible financing options, service and support, and much more.

Kean University
Morris Avenue
Union, NJ 07083
www.kean.edu, (908) 527-2000

COLLEGE PROFILE
Tuition 2002-2003: $5,840
Average Freshman Institutional Aid Award: $6,392
Percent of Students who Receive Freshman Institutional Aid Award: 43%
Average Student Loan: $3,266
Undergraduate Enrollment - Fall 2001: 9,467
Average Class Size: 21
Demographics of Student Body: African-American 22%, Asian 7%,
   Caucasian 51%, Hispanic 20%
Percent of Students with Transfer-in Credit: 45%
Special Adult Programs: Yes

HOW DOES IT COMPARE?
College Experience:	★★★★★
Market Response:	★★★★
Chance of Getting Out:	★★★
Chance of Getting In:	★★★
Career Development Potential:	★★★★
Total Cost:	Low Tuition
	Longer than Average Time to Graduation

MOST POPULAR AREAS OF STUDY
Major Clusters: Analytical/Computational, Social Sciences
Most Popular Majors: Business Management 24%, Education 22%, Social Sciences 20%

UNIQUE FEATURES
— Kean is a metropolitan, comprehensive, interactive, teaching university. A campus dedicated to the pursuit of excellence in higher education, Kean University supports a student-centered learning environment that nurtures the development of the whole student for rewarding careers, lifelong learning and fulfilling lives in a global society. It maintains a commitment to excellence and equity in enrollment, instruction and administration.

— Kean University has grown to become one of New Jersey's largest institutions of higher learning.

New Jersey City University

2039 Kennedy Boulevard
Jersey City, NJ 07305
www.njcu.edu, (201) 200-2000

COLLEGE PROFILE

Tuition 2002-2003: $5,062
Average Freshman Institutional Aid Award: $1,470
Percent of Students who Receive Freshman Institutional Aid Award: 12%
Average Student Loan: $2,731
Undergraduate Enrollment - Fall 2001: 6,398
Average Class Size: n/a
Demographics of Student Body: African-American 19%, Asian 9%, Caucasian 40%, Hispanic 28%
Percent of Students with Transfer-in Credit: n/a
Special Adult Programs: n/a

HOW DOES IT COMPARE?

College Experience:	★★★
Market Response:	★★★
Chance of Getting Out:	★★
Chance of Getting In:	★★
Career Development Potential:	★★★★
Total Cost:	Low Tuition
	Average Time to Graduation

MOST POPULAR AREAS OF STUDY

Major Clusters:	Analytical/Computational, Social Sciences
Most Popular Majors:	Business Management 22%, Social Sciences 11%, Education 10%

UNIQUE FEATURES

In 1998, Jersey City State College achieved official university status and was renamed New Jersey City University. NJCU was restructured to include three colleges: the College of Education, the College of Professional Studies, and the College of Arts and Sciences, in addition to the divisions of Graduate Studies and Continuing Education.

Seton Hall University
400 South Orange Avenue
South Orange, NJ 07079
www.shu.edu, (973) 761-9000

COLLEGE PROFILE
Tuition 2002-2003: $19,400
Average Freshman Institutional Aid Award: $7,544
Percent of Students who Receive Freshman Institutional Aid Award: 76%
Average Student Loan: $3,269
Undergraduate Enrollment - Fall 2001: 5,403
Average Class Size: 20
Demographics of Student Body: African-American 10%, Asian 6%, Caucasian 49%, Hispanic 9%
Percent of Students with Transfer-in Credit: 21%
Special Adult Programs: Yes

HOW DOES IT COMPARE?
College Experience: ★★★★
Market Response: ★★★★★
Chance of Getting Out: ★★
Chance of Getting In: ★
Career Development Potential: ★★★
Total Cost: High Tuition
                   Average Time to Graduation

MOST POPULAR AREAS OF STUDY
Major Clusters: Analytical/Computational, Social Sciences
Most Popular Majors: Business Management -22%, Education 10%, Protective Services 10%

UNIQUE FEATURES
Seton Hall is recognized for its innovation in technology-enhanced teaching and learning, and has been awarded the EDUCAUSE Award for Excellence in Campus Networking.

Adelphi University
1 South Avenue
Garden City, NY 11530
www.adelphi.edu, (516) 877-3000

COLLEGE PROFILE
Tuition 2002-2003: $16,210
Average Freshman Institutional Aid Award: $5,853
Percent of Students who Receive Freshman Institutional Aid Award: 70%
Average Student Loan: $4,000
Undergraduate Enrollment - Fall 2001: 3,391
Average Class Size: 24
Demographics of Student Body: African-American 15%, Asian 5%, Caucasian 71%, Hispanic 9%
Percent of Students with Transfer-in Credit: 43%
Special Adult Programs: Yes

HOW DOES IT COMPARE?
College Experience: ★★★
Market Response: ★★★★
Chance of Getting Out: ★★★
Chance of Getting In: ★★
Career Development Potential: ★★
Total Cost: High Tuition
                     Average Time to Graduation

MOST POPULAR AREAS OF STUDY
Major Clusters: Analytical/Computational, Social Sciences
Most Popular Majors: Business Management 29%, Health Professions 13%
                         Education 11%

UNIQUE FEATURES
— The hub of Adelphi University's new technology infrastructure is the "Information Commons," an expanded center for information services and academic computing, which is located in the University's library.

— Adelphi's 180-bed, resort-style residence hall opens in summer 2003.

Canisius College
2001 Main Street
Buffalo, NY 14208
www.canisius.edu, (716) 833-7000

COLLEGE PROFILE
Tuition 2002-2003: $18,264
Average Freshman Institutional Aid Award: $7,033
Percent of Students who Receive Freshman Institutional Aid Award: 92%
Average Student Loan: $3,994
Undergraduate Enrollment - Fall 2001: 3,378
Average Class Size: 25
Demographics of Student Body: African-American 6%, Hispanic 3%, Asian 1%, Caucasian 75%
Percent of Students with Transfer-in Credit: 31%
Special Adult Programs: Yes

HOW DOES IT COMPARE?
College Experience: ★★★★
Market Response: ★★★★
Chance of Getting Out: ★★★
Chance of Getting In: ★
Career Development Potential: ★★★★
Total Cost: High Tuition
Average Time to Graduation

MOST POPULAR AREAS OF STUDY
Major Clusters: Analytical/Computational, Social Sciences
Most Popular Majors: Education 19%, Biological Sciences 16%, Social Sciences 16%

UNIQUE FEATURES
— In 2001, 100 percent of Canisius College pre-law, pre-medical and pre-dental students were accepted into professional schools.

— In June 2000, the Imagine Canisius capital campaign concluded with over $39 million raised, surpassing the goal for the campaign by $9 million.

City University of New York — Staten Island

2800 Victory Blvd.
Staten Island, NY 10314
www.csi.cuny.edu, (718) 982-2000

COLLEGE PROFILE
Tuition 2002-2003: $3,200
Average Freshman Institutional Aid Award: $1,134
Percent of Students who Receive Freshman Institutional Aid Award: 14%
Average Student Loan: $1,315
Undergraduate Enrollment - Fall 2001: 9,918
Average Class Size: 27
Demographics of Student Body: African-American 11%, Asian 9%, Caucasian 71%, Hispanic 9%
Percent of Students with Transfer-in Credit: 23%
Special Adult Programs: Yes

HOW DOES IT COMPARE?
College Experience: ★★★
Market Response: ★★★★
Chance of Getting Out: ★★★★
Chance of Getting In: ★★★★★
Career Development Potential: ★★
Total Cost: Low Tuition
Longer than Average Time to Graduation

MOST POPULAR AREAS OF STUDY
Major Clusters: Analytical/Computational, Social Sciences
Most Popular Majors: Marketing 23%, Business Management 18%, Social Sciences 17%

UNIQUE FEATURES
— CSI is home to a forward-thinking collaborative program with the NYC Board of Education, the Discovery Institute, which is a model of teacher empowerment strategies for NYC.

— CSI offers 35 academic programs and 15 graduate degree programs, as well as challenging doctoral programs in cooperation with the CUNY Graduate Center.

College of Mount Saint Vincent
6301 Riverdale Avenue
Bronx, NY 10471
www.cmsv.edu, (718) 405-3200

COLLEGE PROFILE
Tuition 2002-2003: $17,880
Average Freshman Institutional Aid Award: $5,800
Percent of Students who Receive Freshman Institutional Aid Award: 89%
Average Student Loan: $2,625
Undergraduate Enrollment - Fall 2001: 1,202
Average Class Size: 20
Demographics of Student Body: African-American 18%, Asian 8%, Caucasian 35%, Hispanic 31%
Percent of Students with Transfer-in Credit: 34%
Special Adult Programs: Yes

HOW DOES IT COMPARE?
College Experience: ★★
Market Response: ★★★★
Chance of Getting Out: ★★
Chance of Getting In: ★
Career Development Potential: ★★★★
Total Cost: High Tuition
Shorter than Average Time to Graduation

MOST POPULAR AREAS OF STUDY
Major Clusters: Quantitative, Social Sciences
Most Popular Majors: Health Professions 38%, Education 10%, Business Management 10%

UNIQUE FEATURES
— An independent, four-year liberal arts college for men and women.

— Few things enhance the value of a college education like the real-world experience gained in an internship. Students at Mount St. Vincent have a double advantage—the College's proximity to the vast number of internship sites available in the greater New York City metropolitan area and the care the school takes to ensure that each internship is a high-quality learning experience.

College of New Rochelle

29 Castle Place
New Rochelle, NY 10805
www.cnr.edu, (914) 632-5300

COLLEGE PROFILE
Tuition 2002-2003: $13,000
Average Freshman Institutional Aid Award: $3,269
Percent of Students who Receive Freshman Institutional Aid Award: 19%
Average Student Loan: $3,927
Undergraduate Enrollment - Fall 2001: 5,123
Average Class Size: 15
Demographics of Student Body: African-American 66%, Asian 1%, Caucasian 18%, Hispanic 15%
Percent of Students with Transfer-in Credit: 27%
Special Adult Programs: Yes

HOW DOES IT COMPARE?
College Experience: ★★★
Market Response: ★★★★
Chance of Getting Out: ★★★★
Chance of Getting In: ★★
Career Development Potential: ★★★★
Total Cost: High Tuition
Shorter than Average Time to Graduation

MOST POPULAR AREAS OF STUDY
Major Clusters: Verbal, Quantitative
Most Popular Majors: Liberal Arts 80%, Health Professions 7%, Psychology 4%

UNIQUE FEATURES
— At the College of New Rochelle students can find diverse and innovative academic programs, extracurricular activities, and a dedicated faculty and staff who are committed to providing an academic experience that will equip them for future success.

— Offering a baccalaureate program designed for adults over 21 years of age where life experience is incorporated directly into the curriculum, the School of New Resources brings the educational experience directly into the community where adults live and work through its seven branch campuses in New Rochelle and throughout New York City.

College of Saint Rose
432 Western Avenue
Albany, NY 12203
www.strose.edu, (518) 454-5111

COLLEGE PROFILE
Tuition 2002-2003: $14,244
Average Freshman Institutional Aid Award: $5,058
Percent of Students who Receive Freshman Institutional Aid Award: 94%
Average Student Loan: $3,212
Undergraduate Enrollment - Fall 2001: 2,726
Average Class Size: 15
Demographics of Student Body: African-American 3%, Asian 1%, Caucasian 84%, Hispanic 2%
Percent of Students with Transfer-in Credit: 58%
Special Adult Programs: Yes

HOW DOES IT COMPARE?
College Experience: ★★★★
Market Response: ★★★★
Chance of Getting Out: ★★★★
Chance of Getting In: ★★
Career Development Potential: ★★★
Total Cost: High Tuition
              Shorter than Average Time to Graduation

MOST POPULAR AREAS OF STUDY
Major Clusters: Social Sciences, Analytical/Computational
Most Popular Majors: Education 50%, Business Management 11%, Social Sciences 6%

UNIQUE FEATURES
—For the past three years, the Saint Rose Graphic Design Program has been named as one of the top ten graphic design programs in the country, by the Art Directors Club of New York, based on a review of student portfolios.

— The Experiences Adult Program (EAP) provides a student with the opportunity to earn credits through portfolio evaluation, for applicable college-level learning experiences acquired outside the traditional classroom.

D'Youville College
320 Porter Avenue
Buffalo, NY 14201
www.dyc.edu, (716) 881-3200

COLLEGE PROFILE
Tuition 2002-2003: $12,550
Average Freshman Institutional Aid Award: $3,663
Percent of Students who Receive Freshman Institutional Aid Award: 80%
Average Student Loan: $4,330
Undergraduate Enrollment - Fall 2001: 976
Average Class Size: 20
Demographics of Student Body: African-American 10%, Asian 2%, Caucasian 66%, Hispanic 4%, Native American 1%
Percent of Students with Transfer-in Credit: 100%
Special Adult Programs: Yes

HOW DOES IT COMPARE?
College Experience:	★★★★
Market Response:	★★
Chance of Getting Out:	★★★
Chance of Getting In:	★★★
Career Development Potential:	★★★

Total Cost: Average Tuition
Longer than Average Time to Graduation

MOST POPULAR AREAS OF STUDY
Major Clusters: Quantitative, Analytical/Computational
Most Popular Majors: Health Professions 70%, Business Management 8%, Home Economics 7%

UNIQUE FEATURES
—The college provides academic programs to approximately 2,400 graduate and undergraduate students in day, evening, weekend and summer sessions.

— Adult Completion Program in Business Management for students who want to complete their degree in 10 months by taking classes one evening per week.

Hofstra University

100 Hofstra University Drive
Hempstead, NY 11549
www.hofstra.edu, (516) 463-6600

COLLEGE PROFILE

Tuition 2002-2003: $15,722
Average Freshman Institutional Aid Award: $3,326
Percent of Students who Receive Freshman Institutional Aid Award: 60%
Average Student Loan: $2,742
Undergraduate Enrollment - Fall 2001: 9,346
Average Class Size: n/a
Demographics of Student Body: African-American 9%, Asian 5%, Caucasian 56%, Hispanic 6%
Percent of Students with Transfer-in Credit: 10%
Special Adult Programs: Yes

HOW DOES IT COMPARE?

College Experience: ★★★
Market Response: ★★★★
Chance of Getting Out: ★★★
Chance of Getting In: ★★
Career Development Potential: ★★★
Total Cost: High Tuition
Average Time to Graduation

MOST POPULAR AREAS OF STUDY

Major Clusters: Social Sciences, Analytical/Computational
Most Popular Majors: Business Management 22%, Psychology 14%, Social Sciences 9%

UNIQUE FEATURES

— New Opportunities at Hofstra (NOAH) — for NY State residents only — provides exceptional support for students who are educationally and financially disadvantaged.

— University Without Walls (UWW) for adults who can spend very little time on campus but whose life situations provide opportunity for full– or part-time learning.

Le Moyne College
1419 Salt Springs Road
Syracuse, NY 13214
www.lemoyne.edu, (315) 445-4100

COLLEGE PROFILE
Tuition 2002-2003: $17,410
Average Freshman Institutional Aid Award: $6,809
Percent of Students who Receive Freshman Institutional Aid Award: 85%
Average Student Loan: $3,356
Undergraduate Enrollment - Fall 2001: 2,445
Average Class Size: 20
Demographics of Student Body: African-American 4%, Asian 2%, Caucasian 83%, Hispanic 3%, Native American 1%
Percent of Students with Transfer-in Credit: 23%
Special Adult Programs: Yes

HOW DOES IT COMPARE?
College Experience: ★★★
Market Response: ★★★★
Chance of Getting Out: ★★★★
Chance of Getting In: ★★
Career Development Potential: ★★★
Total Cost: High Tuition
Shorter than Average Time to Graduation

MOST POPULAR AREAS OF STUDY
Major Clusters: Analytical/Computational, Social Sciences
Most Popular Majors: Business Management 34%, Psychology 20%
Social Sciences 17%

UNIQUE FEATURES
— Le Moyne College is a diverse learning community that strives for academic excellence through its comprehensive programs rooted in the liberal arts and sciences.

— Offers residential Living/Learning Communities for students that provide academic, spiritual, and student support

Manhattan College

4513 Manhattan College Parkway
Riverdale, NY, 10471
www.manhattan.edu, (718) 862-8000

COLLEGE PROFILE
Tuition 2002-2003: $17,100
Average Freshman Institutional Aid Award: $6,750
Percent of Students who Receive Freshman Institutional Aid Award: 85%
Average Student Loan: $4,602
Undergraduate Enrollment - Fall 2001: 2,568
Average Class Size: 20
Demographics of Student Body: African-American 7%, Asian 6%, Caucasian 64%, Hispanic 16%
Percent of Students with Transfer-in Credit: 25%
Special Adult Programs: Yes

HOW DOES IT COMPARE?
College Experience: ★★★★
Market Response: ★★★★
Chance of Getting Out: ★★★
Chance of Getting In: ★
Career Development Potential: ★★★
Total Cost: High Tuition
               Shorter than Average Time to Graduation

MOST POPULAR AREAS OF STUDY
Major Clusters: Applied Quantitative, Analytical/Computational
Most Popular Majors: Engineering 18%, Business Management 16%, Education 16%

UNIQUE FEATURES
From its beginning, Manhattan College paid particular attention to educating first-generation college students, and was an early proponent of access to minority students, establishing special scholarship funds for minority students as early as 1938. Currently, over 30% of the student body are from racial and ethnic minority backgrounds.

Marymount College— Tarrytown

100 Marymount Avenue
Tarrytown, NY 10591
www.marymt.edu, (914) 631-3200

COLLEGE PROFILE
Tuition 2002-2003: $16,680
Average Freshman Institutional Aid Award: $8,837
Percent of Students who Receive Freshman Institutional Aid Award: 90%
Average Student Loan: $3,227
Undergraduate Enrollment - Fall 2001: 938
Average Class Size: 20
Demographics of Student Body: African-American 15%, Asian 5%, Caucasian 37%, Hispanic 16%
Percent of Students with Transfer-in Credit: 44%
Special Adult Programs: Yes

HOW DOES IT COMPARE?
College Experience: ★★★★
Market Response: ★★★
Chance of Getting Out: ★★
Chance of Getting In: ★★★★
Career Development Potential: ★★★★
Total Cost: High Tuition
Shorter than Average Time to Graduation

MOST POPULAR AREAS OF STUDY
Major Clusters: Fine Arts, Analytical/Computational
Most Popular Majors: Business Management 27%, Education 15%, Visual and Performing Arts 12%

UNIQUE FEATURES
If you're a working adult, you can take advantage of personalized attention and distinguished faculty members in a flexible weekend format that accommodates your busy schedule.

Marymount Manhattan College
221 East 71st Street
New York, NY 10021
www.marymount.edu, (212) 517-0400

COLLEGE PROFILE
Tuition 2002-2003: $14,850
Average Freshman Institutional Aid Award: $4,952
Percent of Students who Receive Freshman Institutional Aid Award: 96%
Average Student Loan: $3,571
Undergraduate Enrollment - Fall 2001: 2,707
Average Class Size: 20
Demographics of Student Body: African-American 20%, Asian 4%,
    Hispanic 16%, Caucasian 54%
Percent of Students with Transfer-in Credit: 30%
Special Adult Programs: Yes

HOW DOES IT COMPARE?
College Experience: ★★★
Market Response: ★★★★
Chance of Getting Out: ★★
Chance of Getting In: ★★
Career Development Potential: ★★★
Total Cost: High Tuition
                       Shorter than Average Time to Graduation

MOST POPULAR AREAS OF STUDY
Major Clusters: Analytical/Computational, Social Sciences
Most Popular Majors: Visual & Performing Arts 33%,
                       Business Management 13%, Communications 13%

UNIQUE FEATURES
— Marymount takes advantage of its proximity to the nation's capital through internships, coursework, and guest lecturers who reflect the richness of metropolitan Washington.

— President's Prep Program: Designed for adults who have been away from college for a while and would like a course to assist them in the transition.

Mount Saint Mary College
330 Powell Avenue
Newburgh, NY 12550
www.msmc.edu, (914) 561-0800

COLLEGE PROFILE
Tuition 2002-2003: $12,930
Average Freshman Institutional Aid Award: $2,905
Percent of Students who Receive Freshman Institutional Aid Award: 56%
Average Student Loan: $3,060
Undergraduate Enrollment - Fall 2001: 1,694
Average Class Size: 20
Demographics of Student Body: African-American 10%, Asian 2%, Caucasian 79%, Hispanic 8%
Percent of Students with Transfer-in Credit: 28%
Special Adult Programs: Yes

HOW DOES IT COMPARE?
College Experience: ★★★
Market Response: ★★★
Chance of Getting Out: ★★
Chance of Getting In: ★★★
Career Development Potential: ★★★★
Total Cost: Average Tuition
                     Shorter than Average Time to Graduation

MOST POPULAR AREAS OF STUDY
Major Clusters: Analytical/Computational, Verbal
Most Popular Majors: Business Management 25%, Social Sciences 12%
                       Health Professions 10%

UNIQUE FEATURES
MSMC offers a rich liberal arts education... affordability...an ideal location in the Northeast...individual attention...state of the art technology...a rich experience for both residents and commuters.

Nazareth College of Rochester

4245 East Avenue
Rochester, NY 14618
www.naz.edu, (585) 389-2525

COLLEGE PROFILE
Tuition 2002-2003: $15,910
Average Freshman Institutional Aid Award: $5,451
Percent of Students who Receive Freshman Institutional Aid Award: 85%
Average Student Loan: $4,533
Undergraduate Enrollment - Fall 2001: 1,924
Average Class Size: 25
Demographics of Student Body: African-American 3%, Asian 1%, Caucasian 91%, Hispanic 2%, Native American 1%
Percent of Students with Transfer-in Credit: 33%
Special Adult Programs: Yes

HOW DOES IT COMPARE?
College Experience: ★★★★
Market Response: ★★★★
Chance of Getting Out: ★★★★
Chance of Getting In: ★★
Career Development Potential: ★★★★
Total Cost: High Tuition
Shorter than Average Time to Graduation

MOST POPULAR AREAS OF STUDY
Major Clusters: Social Sciences, Quantitative
Most Popular Majors: Education 18%, Health Professions 14%, Business Management 13%

UNIQUE FEATURES
Nazareth graduate students tutor local school children in the college's Graduate Learning Clinic (GLC). The clinic is part of a six-credit course titled "Practicum in Special Education."

New York Institute of Technology

Northern Blvd.
Old Westbury, NY 11568
www.nyit.edu, (516) 686-7516

COLLEGE PROFILE
Tuition 2002-2003: $15,700
Average Freshman Institutional Aid Award: $7,064
Percent of Students who Receive Freshman Institutional Aid Award: 92%
Average Student Loan: $5,965
Undergraduate Enrollment - Fall 2001: 3,061
Average Class Size: 16
Demographics of Student Body: Caucasian 39%, African-American 9%, Hispanic 5%
Percent of Students with Transfer-in Credit: 11%
Special Adult Programs: Yes

HOW DOES IT COMPARE?
College Experience: ★★★★
Market Response: ★★★★
Chance of Getting Out: ★★
Chance of Getting In: ★★
Career Development Potential: ★★★★
Total Cost: High Tuition
Longer than Average Time to Graduation

MOST POPULAR AREAS OF STUDY
Major Clusters: Analytical/Computational, Quantitative
Most Popular Majors: Business Management 12%, Health Professions 12%, Engineering 11%

UNIQUE FEATURES
—New York Institute of Technology has been a leader in career-focused education, access to opportunity and applications-oriented research since its founding in 1955.

— The Online Campus of New York Institute of Technology is an innovative "virtual campus." Students can take courses, earn certificates, or obtain a four-year college degree through web-based computer conferencing with no campus residency required.

Pratt Institute
200 Willoughby Avenue
Brooklyn, NY 11205
www.pratt.edu, (718) 636-3600

COLLEGE PROFILE
Tuition 2002-2003: $22,196
Average Freshman Institutional Aid Award: $13,680
Percent of Students who Receive Freshman Institutional Aid Award: 92%
Average Student Loan: $3,340
Undergraduate Enrollment - Fall 2001: 3,020
Average Class Size: n/a
Demographics of Student Body: African-American 7%, Asian 23%, Caucasian 64%, Hispanic 7%
Percent of Students with Transfer-in Credit: n/a
Special Adult Programs: n/a

HOW DOES IT COMPARE?
College Experience: ★★★
Market Response: ★★★★★
Chance of Getting Out: ★★★
Chance of Getting In: ★
Career Development Potential: ★★
Total Cost: High Tuition
Shorter than Average Time to Graduation

MOST POPULAR AREAS OF STUDY
Major Clusters: Fine Arts, Applied Quantitative
Most Popular Majors: Architecture 13%, Graphic Design 9%, Industrial Design 5%

UNIQUE FEATURES
Pratt Institute has joined with Munson-Williams-Proctor Institute School of Art to create an exciting educational opportunity, Pratt at Munson-Williams-Proctor. Spend the first two years of your BFA degree on the beautiful Central New York State campus and the remainder of your BFA on the Pratt Brooklyn campus in exciting New York City.

Siena College
515 Loudon Road
Loudonville, NY 12211
www.siena.edu, (518) 783-2300

COLLEGE PROFILE
Tuition 2002-2003: $16,405
Average Freshman Institutional Aid Award: $7,317
Percent of Students who Receive Freshman Institutional Aid Award: 75%
Average Student Loan: $3,890
Undergraduate Enrollment - Fall 2001: 3,379
Average Class Size: 14
Demographics of Student Body: African-American 2%, Asian 2%, Caucasian 93%, Hispanic 2%
Percent of Students with Transfer-in Credit: 4%
Special Adult Programs: Yes

HOW DOES IT COMPARE?
College Experience: ★★★★
Market Response: ★★★★
Chance of Getting Out: ★★★★
Chance of Getting In: ★
Career Development Potential: ★★★★
Total Cost: High Tuition
Shorter than Average Time to Graduation

MOST POPULAR AREAS OF STUDY
Major Clusters: Analytical/Computational
Most Popular Majors: Marketing 23%, Business Management 18%, Social Sciences 17%

UNIQUE FEATURES
— Located in Loudonville on 155 acres, Siena is just two miles north of Albany, New York State's capital city.

— Twenty-five academic majors are available through Siena's three schools: the School of Liberal Arts, School of Business and School of Science.

—Siena also offers special connections such as a joint BA/MD degree program with Albany Medical College, a BSW/MSW agreement with New York University, a Pre-Law program, and Cooperative Engineering programs.

St. Francis College
180 Remson
Brooklyn Heights, NY 11201
www.stfranciscollege.edu, (718) 489-5200

COLLEGE PROFILE
Tuition 2002-2003: $9,450
Average Freshman Institutional Aid Award: $2,564
Percent of Students who Receive Freshman Institutional Aid Award: 62%
Average Student Loan: $3,737
Undergraduate Enrollment - Fall 2001: 2,304
Average Class Size: n/a
Demographics of Student Body: African-American 19%, Asian 3%, Caucasian 52%, Hispanic 14%
Percent of Students with Transfer-in Credit: n/a
Special Adult Programs: Yes

HOW DOES IT COMPARE?
College Experience: ★★★
Market Response: ★★★★
Chance of Getting Out: ★★
Chance of Getting In: ★★★★
Career Development Potential: ★★★
Total Cost: Average Tuition
                    Longer than Average Time to Graduation

MOST POPULAR AREAS OF STUDY
Major Clusters: Analytical/Computational, Verbal
Most Popular Majors: Business Management 30%, Liberal Arts 19%, Social Sciences 13%

UNIQUE FEATURES
St. Francis is an urban school attended primarily by residents of the metropolitan New York area and has strived over the years to be responsive to the city's multiracial, ethnically-varied population, while challenging all students to think in ethical and moral terms and reach beyond academic success to find truths for their personal lives.

148 // Great Colleges for the Real World

St. John Fisher College
3690 East Avenue
Rochester, NY 14618
www.sjfc.edu, (716) 385-8000

COLLEGE PROFILE
Tuition 2002-2003: $15,400
Average Freshman Institutional Aid Award: $2,516
Percent of Students who Receive Freshman Institutional Aid Award: 76%
Average Student Loan: $2,254
Undergraduate Enrollment - Fall 2001: 2,175
Average Class Size: 20
Demographics of Student Body: African-American 5%, Asian 1%, Caucasian 87%, Hispanic 3%
Percent of Students with Transfer-in Credit: n/a
Special Adult Programs: Yes

HOW DOES IT COMPARE?
College Experience: ★★
Market Response: ★★★★
Chance of Getting Out: ★★★★
Chance of Getting In: ★★★★
Career Development Potential: ★★
Total Cost: High Tuition
                    Shorter than Average Time to Graduation

MOST POPULAR AREAS OF STUDY
Major Clusters: Analytical/Computational, Social Sciences
Most Popular Majors: Business Management 29%, Social Sciences 15%, Psychology 11%

UNIQUE FEATURES
— Five Fisher faculty members have received prestigious Fulbright Scholarships, an honor accorded to only about one thousand faculty members in the nation each year. Also, the John Templeton Foundation named Fisher to its 1999-2000 Honor Roll for Character-Building Colleges, an honor extended to fewer than five percent of all colleges in the United States.

— 95 percent of students enter graduate school or accept employment offers within one year of graduation.

St. Thomas Aquinas College
125 Route 340
Sparkill, NY 10976
www.stac.edu, (845) 398-4000

COLLEGE PROFILE
Tuition 2002-2003: $13,780
Average Freshman Institutional Aid Award: $2,586
Percent of Students who Receive Freshman Institutional Aid Award: 75%
Average Student Loan: $2,482
Undergraduate Enrollment - Fall 2001: 1,949
Average Class Size: 18
Demographics of Student Body: African-American 5%, Asian 4%, Caucasian 74%, Hispanic 10%
Percent of Students with Transfer-in Credit: 35%
Special Adult Programs: Yes

HOW DOES IT COMPARE?
College Experience: ★★★★
Market Response: ★★★
Chance of Getting Out: ★★★
Chance of Getting In: ★★
Career Development Potential: ★★★★
Total Cost: High Tuition
Shorter than Average Time to Graduation

MOST POPULAR AREAS OF STUDY
Major Clusters: Analytical/Computational, Social Sciences
Most Popular Majors: Business Management 23%, Education 16%, Social Sciences 12%

UNIQUE FEATURES
St. Thomas Aquinas College has the people and programs to help students get to where they want to be in the twenty-first century. The college offers three masters degrees, thirty-one baccalaureate majors, two associate degrees, certificate programs and dual degrees in Physical Therapy, Engineering, Business, Education and many more.

State University of New York — Maritime College

6 Pennyfield Avenue
Throggs Neck, NY 10465
www.sunymaritime.edu, (718) 409-7200

COLLEGE PROFILE
Tuition 2002-2003: $5,215
Average Freshman Institutional Aid Award: $2,595
Percent of Students who Receive Freshman Institutional Aid Award: 29%
Average Student Loan: $2,628
Undergraduate Enrollment - Fall 2001: 622
Average Class Size: 19
Demographics of Student Body: African-American 7%, Asian 3%, Caucasian 79%, Hispanic 6%
Percent of Students with Transfer-in Credit: 25%
Special Adult Programs: Yes

HOW DOES IT COMPARE?
College Experience: ★★★
Market Response: ★★★★
Chance of Getting Out: ★★★★
Chance of Getting In: ★★
Career Development Potential: ★★★★★
Total Cost: Low Tuition
             Average Time to Graduation

MOST POPULAR AREAS OF STUDY
Major Clusters: Applied Quantitative, Analytical/Computational
Most Popular Majors: Engineering 48%, Business Management 43%, Physical Sciences 9%

UNIQUE FEATURES
— Maritime College graduates step out of the classroom and into positions of immediate responsibility in industry, government, the military, or other pursuits of their choice.

— The College experiences 100% career placement of its graduating seniors.

State University of New York — Oswego

Oswego, NY 13126
www.oswego.edu, (315) 312-2500

COLLEGE PROFILE
Tuition 2002-2003: $3,400
Average Freshman Institutional Aid Award: $868
Percent of Students who Receive Freshman Institutional Aid Award: 17%
Average Student Loan: $2,711
Undergraduate Enrollment - Fall 2001: 7,062
Average Class Size: 28
Demographics of Student Body: African-American 4%, Asian 2%, Caucasian 90%, Hispanic 3%, Native American 1%
Percent of Students with Transfer-in Credit: 38%
Special Adult Programs: Yes

HOW DOES IT COMPARE?
College Experience: ★★★
Market Response: ★★
Chance of Getting Out: ★★★★★
Chance of Getting In: ★★★
Career Development Potential: ★★
Total Cost: Low Tuition
Shorter than Average Time to Graduation

MOST POPULAR AREAS OF STUDY
Major Clusters: Analytical/Computational, Social Sciences
Most Popular Majors: Education 29%, Business Management 21%, Communication 10%

UNIQUE FEATURES
In any journey, the first step is the most important. That's why SUNY Oswego has developed FirstChoice, an exciting new option for first-year students. With FirstChoice, students will be in a small class setting, and have a chance to really get to know their professors, make new friends, and learn about Oswego. Students will develop the skills they need to succeed in college and start planning for their future.

Wells College
Route 90
Aurora, NY 13026
www.wells.edu, (315) 364-3266

COLLEGE PROFILE
Tuition 2002-2003: $13,070
Average Freshman Institutional Aid Award: $6,200
Percent of Students who Receive Freshman Institutional Aid Award: 88%
Average Student Loan: $4,375
Undergraduate Enrollment - Fall 2001: 443
Average Class Size: 12
Demographics of Student Body: African-American 5%, Asian 4%, Caucasian 79%, Hispanic 4%
Percent of Students with Transfer-in Credit: 25%
Special Adult Programs: No

HOW DOES IT COMPARE?
College Experience: ★★
Market Response: ★★★★
Chance of Getting Out: ★★★★
Chance of Getting In: ★★★
Career Development Potential: ★★
Total Cost: High Tuition
                    Shorter than Average Time to Graduation

MOST POPULAR AREAS OF STUDY
Major Clusters: Social Sciences
Most Popular Majors: Psychology 19%, Biological Sciences 13%, Interdisciplinary 9%

UNIQUE FEATURES
— Wells students prepare for careers and entrance into top graduate and professional schools through experiential learning: internships, research with faculty members, community service, and other options. 92% of the women in Wells' Class of 2001 held at least one internship during their college years.

— Wells offers education of the highest quality at an affordable price. This impressive combination makes us a best value among national liberal arts colleges.

Johnson C. Smith University

100-152 Beatties Ford Road
Charlotte, NC 28216
www.jcsu.edu, (704) 378-1000

College Profile
Tuition 2002-2003: $12,444
Average Freshman Institutional Aid Award: $2,407
Percent of Students who Receive Freshman Institutional Aid Award: 17%
Average Student Loan: $6,000
Undergraduate Enrollment - Fall 2001: 1,595
Average Class Size: 20
Demographics of Student Body: African-American 99%, Asian 1%
Percent of Students with Transfer-in Credit: 3%
Special Adult Programs: Yes

HOW DOES IT COMPARE?

College Experience: ★★
Market Response: ★★★
Chance of Getting Out: ★★★★
Chance of Getting In: ★★★★
Career Development Potential: ★★
Total Cost: Average Tuition
                   Longer than Average Time to Graduation

MOST POPULAR AREAS OF STUDY

Major Clusters: Analytical/Computational, Social Sciences
Most Popular Majors: Business Management 21%, Computer & Information Sciences 16%, Social Sciences 8%

UNIQUE FEATURES

—The Golden Bull Academy is for students who already have been accepted to the University. It gives students and parents an opportunity to learn about educational opportunities and expectations at JCSU. During this weekend visit to the campus, students and parents have an opportunity to register early for classes, learn about chosen or potential majors, and get a glimpse of student life.

— JCSU is the first Historically Black IBM ThinkPad University. Students and their school-provided laptops will have complete access to the school's campus-wide network and Internet services.

Meredith College
3800 Hillsborough Street
Raleigh, NC, 27607
www.meredith.edu, (919) 760-8600

COLLEGE PROFILE
Tuition 2002-2003: $16,465
Average Freshman Institutional Aid Award: $2,950
Percent of Students who Receive Freshman Institutional Aid Award: 44%
Average Student Loan: $4,336
Undergraduate Enrollment - Fall 2001: 2,432
Average Class Size: 20
Demographics of Student Body: African-American 6%, Asian 1%, Caucasian 89%, Hispanic 2%
Percent of Students with Transfer-in Credit: 64%
Special Adult Programs: Yes

HOW DOES IT COMPARE?
College Experience: ★★★
Market Response: ★★★★
Chance of Getting Out: ★★★★
Chance of Getting In: ★★
Career Development Potential: ★★★★
Total Cost: High Tuition
Shorter than Average Time to Graduation

MOST POPULAR AREAS OF STUDY
Major Clusters: Analytical/Computational
Most Popular Majors: Business Management 25%, Visual & Performing Arts 14%, Psychology 11%

UNIQUE FEATURES
—Meredith College's performance exceeds the national average in five critical categories, according to the 2001 National Survey of Student Engagement, a comprehensive assessment of higher education practices.

— Meredith's location is ideal for attracting top-notch faculty and providing internship and co-op opportunities. Raleigh is North Carolina's center for government, culture, business and entertainment

Queens University of Charlotte

1900 Selwyn Avenue
Charlotte, NC 28274
www.queens.edu, (704) 337-2200

COLLEGE PROFILE
Tuition 2002-2003: $12,290
Average Freshman Institutional Aid Award: $4,340
Percent of Students who Receive Freshman Institutional Aid Award: 59%
Average Student Loan: $2,625
Undergraduate Enrollment - Fall 2001: 1,156
Average Class Size: 20
Demographics of Student Body: African-American 15%, Asian 1%, Caucasian 75%, Hispanic 2%
Percent of Students with Transfer-in Credit: 80%
Special Adult Programs: Yes

HOW DOES IT COMPARE?
College Experience: ★★★
Market Response: ★★★
Chance of Getting Out: ★★★★
Chance of Getting In: ★★★
Career Development Potential: ★★★
Total Cost: Average Tuition
Shorter than Average Time to Graduation

MOST POPULAR AREAS OF STUDY
Major Clusters: Analytical/Computational, Quantitative
Most Popular Majors: Business Management 28%, Communications 19% Health Professions 14%

UNIQUE FEATURES

— The Blair House for Internships and Career Programs at Queens University of Charlotte provides an academic forum to help students and alumni translate their liberal arts education into productive careers and noble lives. It challenges individuals to combine their gifts, academic preparation and experience into a lifework plan.

— The McColl Executive MBA is designed to be completed in two calendar years. The Program consists of four regular semesters and two summer semesters. In each semester, concepts from different contexts and disciplines are presented. This integration provides opportunities to put concepts developed in one area to use in another, resulting in a comprehensive and integrated educational experience.

University of North Carolina — Charlotte

9201 University City Blvd.
Charlotte, NC 28223
www.uncc.edu, (704) 687-2000

COLLEGE PROFILE
Tuition 2002-2003: $2,460
Average Freshman Institutional Aid Award: $2,279
Percent of Students who Receive Freshman Institutional Aid Award: 18%
Average Student Loan: $4,969
Undergraduate Enrollment - Fall 2001: 15,135
Average Class Size: 30
Demographics of Student Body: African-American 16%, Asian 5%, Caucasian 73%, Hispanic 2%, Native American 1%
Percent of Students with Transfer-in Credit: 11%
Special Adult Programs: Yes

HOW DOES IT COMPARE?
College Experience: ★★★
Market Response: ★★★
Chance of Getting Out: ★★★
Chance of Getting In: ★★★
Career Development Potential: ★★★★
Total Cost: Low Tuition
Longer than Average Time to Graduation

MOST POPULAR AREAS OF STUDY
Major Clusters: Analytical/Computational, Social Sciences
Most Popular Majors: Business Management 26%, Engineering 10%, Education 7%

UNIQUE FEATURES
— The University of North Carolina-Charlotte uses the metropolitan Charlotte region, which includes 1.5 million residents, as a laboratory in teaching the liberal arts, the basic sciences, engineering, architecture, business, education, and nursing and health professions.

— OASES: Office of Adult Students and Evening Services, serves as a liaison with academic departments, advising center, and administrative offices for students who need to conduct business after normal college hours.

Baldwin Wallace College
275 Eastland Road
Berea, OH 44017
www.bw.edu, (440) 826-2900

COLLEGE PROFILE
Tuition 2002-2003: $17,432
Average Freshman Institutional Aid Award: $6,516
Percent of Students who Receive Freshman Institutional Aid Award: 94%
Average Student Loan: $3,326
Undergraduate Enrollment - Fall 2001: 3,993
Average Class Size: 20
Demographics of Student Body: African-American 4%, Asian 1%, Caucasian 85%, Hispanic 17%
Percent of Students with Transfer-in Credit: 95%
Special Adult Programs: Yes

HOW DOES IT COMPARE?
College Experience:	★★★★
Market Response:	★★★
Chance of Getting Out:	★★★
Chance of Getting In:	★★★
Career Development Potential:	★★★
Total Cost:	High Tuition
	Shorter than Average Time to Graduation

MOST POPULAR AREAS OF STUDY
Major Clusters: Analytical/Computational, Social Sciences
Most Popular Majors: Business Management 32%, Education 18%, Social Sciences 7%

UNIQUE FEATURES
— Baldwin Wallace offers more than 50 major, 3/2 cooperative, and pre-professional programs in its day programs.

— B-W's Evening and weekend programs offer 12 major and eight certificate programs.

— B-W's affordable tuition ranks among the lowest of private colleges in Ohio. To help students and their families meet the cost of a quality education, B-W awards more than $40 million annually to B-W students in the form of scholarships, grants, loans, and work-study.

Cleveland State University

E. 24th & Euclid Avenue
Cleveland, OH 44115
www.csuohio.edu, (216) 687-2000

COLLEGE PROFILE
Tuition 2002-2003: $5,184
Average Freshman Institutional Aid Award: $2,370
Percent of Students who Receive Freshman Institutional Aid Award: 24%
Average Student Loan: $5,359
Undergraduate Enrollment - Fall 2001: 10,433
Average Class Size: 26
Demographics of Student Body: African-American 19%, Asian 3%,
    Caucasian 61%, Hispanic 3%, Native American 3%
Percent of Students with Transfer-in Credit: 50%
Special Adult Programs: Yes

HOW DOES IT COMPARE?
College Experience: ★★★
Market Response: ★★★
Chance of Getting Out: ★★
Chance of Getting In: ★★★★★
Career Development Potential: ★★★★
Total Cost: Low Tuition
               Longer than Average Time to Graduation

MOST POPULAR AREAS OF STUDY
Major Clusters: Verbal, Social Sciences
Most Popular Majors: Communications 3%, Education 3%,
                       Psychology 2%

UNIQUE FEATURES
— CSU is the most diverse public institution in the State of Ohio and is a national and state leader in preparing and graduating minority students from graduate and professional programs.

— Over the past decade, CSU has built a strong technological platform which enables enhanced support for faculty research and for classroom instruction. Compressed video instruction is offered at ten remote locations in the region, and interactive connections are available worldwide.

College of Mount Saint Joseph

5701 Delhi Road
Cincinnati, OH 45233
www.msj.edu, (513) 244-4200

COLLEGE PROFILE

Tuition 2002-2003: $14,950
Average Freshman Institutional Aid Award: $5,922
Percent of Students who Receive Freshman Institutional Aid Award: 90%
Average Student Loan: $3,425
Undergraduate Enrollment - Fall 2001: 2,071
Average Class Size: 14
Demographics of Student Body: Caucasian 86%, African-American 7%, Hispanic 1%, Asian 2%
Percent of Students with Transfer-in Credit: 38%
Special Adult Programs: Yes

HOW DOES IT COMPARE?

College Experience:	★★★
Market Response:	★★★★
Chance of Getting Out:	★★★★
Chance of Getting In:	★★
Career Development Potential:	★★★★
Total Cost:	High Tuition
	Shorter than Average Time to Graduation

MOST POPULAR AREAS OF STUDY

Major Clusters: Analytical/Computational, Quantitative
Most Popular Majors: Business Management 20%, Education 16%, Health Professions 15%

UNIQUE FEATURES

— At the College of Mount St. Joseph, students won't get the run-around because the Mount adds personal attention, convenience and flexibility to its services. Centralized services in the Thomas L. Conlan Center and online services help students with everything from registration and buying books to checking out financial aid and getting a free parking pass.

— One of the nations' first wireless computing colleges; new full-time students get a laptop fully equipped for wireless use around campus.

DeVry University — Columbus
1350 Alum Creek Drive
Columbus, OH 43209
www.devrycols.edu, (614) 253-7291

COLLEGE PROFILE
Tuition 2002-2003: $9,390
Average Freshman Institutional Aid Award: $2,036
Percent of Students who Receive Freshman Institutional Aid Award: 5%
Average Student Loan: $6,681
Undergraduate Enrollment - Fall 2001: 3,793
Average Class Size: 30
Demographics of Student Body: African-American 20%, Caucasian 74%, Asian 31%, Hispanic 1%
Percent of Students with Transfer-in Credit: 12%
Special Adult Programs: Yes

HOW DOES IT COMPARE?
College Experience: ★★★
Market Response: ★★
Chance of Getting Out: ★★
Chance of Getting In: ★★★★★
Career Development Potential: ★★★
Total Cost: Average Tuition
                     Shorter than Average Time to Graduation

MOST POPULAR AREAS OF STUDY
Major Clusters: Applied Quantitative, Analytical/Computational
Most Popular Majors: Computer Information Sciences 50%,
                      Engineering Technologies 25%,
                      Electronics and Computer Technologies 25%

UNIQUE FEATURES
— Because DeVry's programs target the modern workplace, for the past decade more than 91 percent of DeVry's graduates have landed jobs in education-related fields within six months of graduation.

— DeVry offers Evening College courses for the part-time student population.

Franklin University
201 S. Grant Street
Columbus, OH 43215
www.franklin.edu, (614) 341-6300

COLLEGE PROFILE
Tuition 2002-2003: $6,420
Average Freshman Institutional Aid Award: $2,337
Percent of Students who Receive Freshman Institutional Aid Award: 16%
Average Student Loan: n/a
Undergraduate Enrollment - Fall 2001: 4,650
Average Class Size: 18
Demographics of Student Body: African-American 14%, Asian 3%, Caucasian 69%, Hispanic 1%
Percent of Students with Transfer-in Credit: 73%
Special Adult Programs: Yes

HOW DOES IT COMPARE?
College Experience: ★
Market Response: ★★
Chance of Getting Out: ★★
Chance of Getting In: ★★★★★
Career Development Potential: ★★★
Total Cost: Low Tuition
Average Time to Graduation

MOST POPULAR AREAS OF STUDY
Major Clusters: Analytical/Computational, Quantitative
Most Popular Majors: Business Management 67%,
Computer Information Sciences 16%
Health Professions 9%

UNIQUE FEATURES
— Centennial Celebration: For 100 years, Franklin University has been changing lives by educating the community's working professionals.

— MBA Focuses: Beginning Fall 2002, the MBA will be expanding its available courseware to offer four focuses (leadership, management information systems, finance, and entrepreneurship) that will be available online; the Leadership Focus will also be available on-site.

John Carroll University
20700 North Park Blvd.
Cleveland, OH 44118
www.jcu.edu, (216) 397-1886

COLLEGE PROFILE
Tuition 2002-2003: $18,832
Average Freshman Institutional Aid Award: $7,069
Percent of Students who Receive Freshman Institutional Aid Award: 91%
Average Student Loan: $3,357
Undergraduate Enrollment - Fall 2001: 3,508
Average Class Size: 19
Demographics of Student Body: African-American 5%, Asian 3%, Caucasian 87%, Hispanic 2%
Percent of Students with Transfer-in Credit: 25%
Special Adult Programs: n/a

HOW DOES IT COMPARE?
College Experience: ★★
Market Response: ★★★★
Chance of Getting Out: ★★★
Chance of Getting In: ★
Career Development Potential: ★★★★
Total Cost: High Tuition
Shorter than Average Time to Graduation

MOST POPULAR AREAS OF STUDY
Major Clusters: Analytical/Computational, Social Sciences
Most Popular Majors: Communications 12%, Biology 10%, Psychology 8%,

UNIQUE FEATURES
— The University places primary emphasis on instructional excellence. A faculty not only professionally qualified, but also student oriented, considers excellence in interpersonal relationships as well as academic achievement among its primary goals.

— Opening new state-of-the-art Dolan Science and Technology Center in Fall 2003.

University of Cincinnati
PO Box 210127
Cincinnati, OH 45221
www.uc.edu, (513) 556-6000

COLLEGE PROFILE
Tuition 2002-2003: $5,715
Average Freshman Institutional Aid Award: $3,245
Percent of Students who Receive Freshman Institutional Aid Award: 28%
Average Student Loan: $7,006
Undergraduate Enrollment - Fall 2001: 19,876
Average Class Size: 20
Demographics of Student Body: African-American 12%, Asian 3%, Caucasian 74%, Hispanic 1%
Percent of Students with Transfer-in Credit: 25%
Special Adult Programs: Yes

HOW DOES IT COMPARE?
College Experience: ★★★
Market Response: ★★★
Chance of Getting Out: ★★★
Chance of Getting In: ★★★
Career Development Potential: ★★
Total Cost: Low Tuition
               Longer than Average Time to Graduation

MOST POPULAR AREAS OF STUDY
Major Clusters: Applied Quantitative, Analytical/Computational
Most Popular Majors: Business Management 20%, Engineering 12%, Social Sciences 9%

UNIQUE FEATURES
— The University of Cincinnati invented cooperative education, in which students alternate between classroom instruction and on-the-job learning. UC's "co-op" program is among the largest and most successful in the world.

— The University of Cincinnati is completely renovating its campus, using world-renowned architects while adding a huge student recreation center. *The New York Times* called UC "one of the most architecturally dynamic campuses in America today."

University of Dayton
300 College Park
Dayton, OH 45469
www.udayton.edu, (937) 229-4411

COLLEGE PROFILE
Tuition 2002-2003: $18,000
Average Freshman Institutional Aid Award: $5,826
Percent of Students who Receive Freshman Institutional Aid Award: 87%
Average Student Loan: $4,166
Undergraduate Enrollment - Fall 2001: 7,151
Average Class Size: 28
Demographics of Student Body: African-American 3%, Asian 1%, Caucasian 94%, Hispanic 2%, Native American 1%
Percent of Students with Transfer-in Credit: 28%
Special Adult Programs: Yes

HOW DOES IT COMPARE?
College Experience: ★★★★
Market Response: ★★★★
Chance of Getting Out: ★★★
Chance of Getting In: ★
Career Development Potential: ★★★
Total Cost: High Tuition
Shorter than Average Time to Graduation

MOST POPULAR AREAS OF STUDY
Major Clusters: Analytical/Computational, Social Sciences
Most Popular Majors: Business Management 23%, Engineering 18%, Education 12%

UNIQUE FEATURES
— A residential learning community with more than 70 academic programs in arts and sciences, business administration, education and allied professions, engineering and law.

— Selected by the Templeton Foundation as having one of the nation's best service-learning programs that encourages students to contribute and learn through volunteer activity.

Xavier University

3800 Victory Parkway
Cincinnati, OH 45207
www.xu.edu, (513) 754-3000

COLLEGE PROFILE

Tuition 2002-2003: $17,780
Average Freshman Institutional Aid Award: $6,569
Percent of Students who Receive Freshman Institutional Aid Award: 81%
Average Student Loan: $4,280
Undergraduate Enrollment - Fall 2001: 4,006
Average Class Size: 23
Demographics of Student Body: African-American 9%, Asian 2%, Caucasian 83%, Hispanic 1%
Percent of Students with Transfer-in Credit: 46%
Special Adult Programs: Yes

HOW DOES IT COMPARE?

College Experience:	★★★★
Market Response:	★★★★
Chance of Getting Out:	★★★
Chance of Getting In:	★
Career Development Potential:	★★★★
Total Cost:	High Tuition
	Shorter than Average Time to Graduation

MOST POPULAR AREAS OF STUDY

Major Clusters:	Analytical/Computational, Verbal
Most Popular Majors:	Business Marketing 22%, Liberal Arts 19%, Communications 11%

UNIQUE FEATURES

— Freshman retention rate of 89 percent exceeds the national average of 78 percent for private colleges.

— Accelerated Weekend Degree Programs that allow students to complete four-year degrees in four years or less in liberal arts or business management.

Portland State University

PO Box 751
Portland, OR 751
www.pdx.edu, (503) 725-4433

COLLEGE PROFILE
Tuition 2002-2003: $3,831
Average Freshman Institutional Aid Award: $929
Percent of Students who Receive Freshman Institutional Aid Award: 15%
Average Student Loan: $3,780
Undergraduate Enrollment - Fall 2001: 13,601
Average Class Size: 22
Demographics of Student Body: African-American 3%, Asian 9%, Caucasian 66%, Hispanic 4%, Native American 1%
Percent of Students with Transfer-in Credit: 63%
Special Adult Programs: Yes

HOW DOES IT COMPARE?
College Experience: ★★★
Market Response: ★★★
Chance of Getting Out: ★★
Chance of Getting In: ★★★
Career Development Potential: ★★★
Total Cost: Low Tuition
                  Longer than Average Time to Graduation

MOST POPULAR AREAS OF STUDY
Major Clusters: Analytical/Computational, Social Sciences
Most Popular Majors: Social Sciences 25% Business Management 21%, English Language/Literature 8%

UNIQUE FEATURES

— Portland State University is Oregon's largest and most diverse university, offering over 100 bachelor's, master's, and doctoral programs in areas such as urban studies and planning, computer science, social work, business administration, environmental science, liberal arts, music and education.

— Portland State is home to the nationally-recognized University Studies program, in which students apply classroom theory to the real-world challenges in the Portland-metropolitan community.

—Students have extensive opportunities for co-curricular work in the community as interns and research assistants in the state's largest center for science, engineering, arts, and education.

Get In. Get Out. Get a Job. // 167

University of Portland
5000 N. Willamette Blvd.
Portland, OR 97208
www.up.edu, (503) 943-7911

COLLEGE PROFILE
Tuition 2002-2003: $24,000
Average Freshman Institutional Aid Award: $8,497
Percent of Students who Receive Freshman Institutional Aid Award: 88%
Average Student Loan: $6,158
Undergraduate Enrollment - Fall 2001: 2,512
Average Class Size: n/a
Demographics of Student Body: African-American 1%, Asian 9%, Caucasian 79%, Hispanic 4%
Percent of Students with Transfer-in Credit: 6%
Special Adult Programs: Yes

HOW DOES IT COMPARE?
College Experience:	★★★
Market Response:	★★★★
Chance of Getting Out:	★★★
Chance of Getting In:	★★★
Career Development Potential:	★★
Total Cost:	High Tuition
	Shorter than Average Time to Graduation

MOST POPULAR AREAS OF STUDY
Major Clusters: Applied Quantitative, Analytical/Computational
Most Popular Majors: Business Management 19%, Engineering 13%, Health Professions 12%

UNIQUE FEATURES
Though small in size, the University's resources for its on-campus community are astonishingly vast: 1,100 courses and 72 programs of study; a 350,000-volume library, dozens of computer laboratories offering free software classes; more than 40 student clubs; several offices dedicated to fostering student well being; and specialized services for faculty, staff, and parents.

California University of Pennsylvania
250 University Avenue
California, PA 15419
www.cup.edu, (724) 938-4404

COLLEGE PROFILE
Tuition 2002-2003: $5,473
Average Freshman Institutional Aid Award: $1,463
Percent of Students who Receive Freshman Institutional Aid Award: 11%
Average Student Loan: $2,635
Undergraduate Enrollment - Fall 2001: 5,003
Average Class Size: n/a
Demographics of Student Body: African-American 4%, Caucasian 94%
Percent of Students with Transfer-in Credit: 34%
Special Adult Programs: Yes

HOW DOES IT COMPARE?
College Experience: ★★
Market Response: ★
Chance of Getting Out: ★★★
Chance of Getting In: ★★★★★
Career Development Potential: ★★
Total Cost: Low Tuition
Longer than Average Time to Graduation

MOST POPULAR AREAS OF STUDY
Major Clusters: Analytical/Computational, Social Sciences
Most Popular Majors: Education 30%, Business Management 12%, Social Sciences 7%

UNIQUE FEATURES
The Office of Lifelong Learning, located in the Eberly Science and Technology Center, serves learners interested in both credit and noncredit learning opportunities. The programs of study are flexible and can be customized to meet your desire to further your education. The classes are offered in the evenings and on Saturdays at times intended to accommodate the busy schedules of most adults. The goal is to provide "one-stop" ease in processing your information, registration and any questions you may have.

Chestnut Hill College
9601 Germantown Avenue
Philadelphia, PA 19118
www.chc.edu, (215) 248-7000

COLLEGE PROFILE
Tuition 2002-2003: $17,500
Average Freshman Institutional Aid Award: $8,990
Percent of Students who Receive Freshman Institutional Aid Award: 91%
Average Student Loan: $3,240
Undergraduate Enrollment - Fall 2001: 936
Average Class Size: 20
Demographics of Student Body: African-American 34%, Asian 2%, Caucasian 43%, Hispanic 4%
Percent of Students with Transfer-in Credit: 85%
Special Adult Programs: Yes

HOW DOES IT COMPARE?
College Experience: ★★★★
Market Response: ★★★★
Chance of Getting Out: ★★
Chance of Getting In: ★
Career Development Potential: ★★★
Total Cost: High Tuition
Shorter than Average Time to Graduation

MOST POPULAR AREAS OF STUDY
Major Clusters: Analytical/Computational, Social Sciences
Most Popular Majors: Business Management 22%, Social Sciences 16%
Education 12%

UNIQUE FEATURES
Chestnut Hill ACCELERATED offers alternative delivery of undergraduate degrees in a fast-paced, flexible, efficient format. Six 8-week sessions are offered each year. Courses meet twice a week for two hours and twenty minutes in the evenings, Friday afternoons or evenings, Saturdays mornings or afternoons.

Delaware Valley College
700 E. Butler Avenue
Doylestown, PA 18901
www.devalcol.edu, (215) 345-1500

COLLEGE PROFILE
Tuition 2002-2003: $17,680
Average Freshman Institutional Aid Award: $7,604
Percent of Students who Receive Freshman Institutional Aid Award: 94%
Average Student Loan: $3,290
Undergraduate Enrollment - Fall 2001: 1,900
Average Class Size: 18
Demographics of Student Body: African-American 3%, Asian 1%, Caucasian 77%, Hispanic 2%
Percent of Students with Transfer-in Credit: 80%
Special Adult Programs: Yes

HOW DOES IT COMPARE?
College Experience: ★★★★
Market Response: ★★★
Chance of Getting Out: ★★
Chance of Getting In: ★★★
Career Development Potential: ★★★★
Total Cost: High Tuition
              Shorter than Average Time to Graduation

MOST POPULAR AREAS OF STUDY
Major Clusters: Applied Quantitative, Analytical/Computational
Most Popular Majors: Agricultural Sciences 56%,
                      Business Management 25%,
                      General Sciences 8%

UNIQUE FEATURES
— The Weekend College is designed for busy adults who are working full-time, have family responsibilities, travel frequently, or work at night. Courses are offered Friday evenings, Saturday mornings and afternoons, and Sunday afternoons.

— Hands-on Science is emphasized by laboratories and application of knowledge gained in course work.

Drexel University
3141 Chestnut Street
Philadelphia, PA 19104
www.drexel.edu, (215) 895-2000

COLLEGE PROFILE
Tuition 2002-2003: $17,393
Average Freshman Institutional Aid Award: $7,330
Percent of Students who Receive Freshman Institutional Aid Award: 92%
Average Student Loan: $3,240
Undergraduate Enrollment - Fall 2001: 11,019
Average Class Size: 25
Demographics of Student Body: African-American 8%, Asian 13%, Caucasian 56%, Hispanic 2%
Percent of Students with Transfer-in Credit: 80%
Special Adult Programs: Yes

HOW DOES IT COMPARE?
College Experience: ★★★★★
Market Response: ★★★★★
Chance of Getting Out: ★★
Chance of Getting In: ★
Career Development Potential: ★★★
Total Cost: High Tuition
Longer than Average Time to Graduation

MOST POPULAR AREAS OF STUDY
Major Clusters: Applied Quantitative, Analytical/Computational
Most Popular Majors: Engineering 25%, Business Management 24%, Computer Information Sciences 16%

UNIQUE FEATURES
Drexel University now offers an eleven-month intensive full-time program for people holding bachelor's or master's degrees in other areas who want to become registered nurses (RNs). The program is ideal for college graduates who want to change careers. Students graduate from the Accelerated Career Entry program (ACE) with a Bachelor of Science in Nursing in just eleven months, rather than the more traditional three or four years. This program is ideal for working adults or college graduates who want to change careers and do it in one year.

Eastern College

1300 Eagle Road
St. Davids, PA 19087
www.eastern.edu, (610) 341-5800

COLLEGE PROFILE
Tuition 2002-2003: $15,832
Average Freshman Institutional Aid Award: $5,946
Percent of Students who Receive Freshman Institutional Aid Award: 98%
Average Student Loan: $4,095
Undergraduate Enrollment - Fall 2001: 1,942
Average Class Size: 20
Demographics of Student Body: African-American 18%, Asian 2%, Caucasian 74%, Hispanic 4%
Percent of Students with Transfer-in Credit: 15%
Special Adult Programs: Yes

HOW DOES IT COMPARE?
College Experience: ★
Market Response: ★★★
Chance of Getting Out: ★★★
Chance of Getting In: ★★
Career Development Potential: ★★
Total Cost: High Tuition
              Average Time to Graduation

MOST POPULAR AREAS OF STUDY
Major Clusters: Analytical/Computational, Social Sciences
Most Popular Majors: Business Management 50%, Education 9%, Theological Studies 8%

UNIQUE FEATURES
— The School of Professional Studies offers programs that are appropriate to the learning needs of adults, respectful of the life experiences of adults, and sensitive to the multifaceted lives of adults.

— Eastern University offers the Fast Track MBA experience as a package: A group of approximately 20 students travel together through the program, taking sequential courses.

Gwynedd-Mercy College

Sumneytown Pike, Box 901
Gwynedd Valley, PA 19437
www.gmc.edu, (215) 646-7300

COLLEGE PROFILE
Tuition 2002-2003: $15,600
Average Freshman Institutional Aid Award: $6,420
Percent of Students who Receive Freshman Institutional Aid Award: 87%
Average Student Loan: $3,007
Undergraduate Enrollment - Fall 2001: 1,900
Average Class Size: 19
Demographics of Student Body: African-American 11%, Hispanic 2%, Caucasian 82%, Asian 3%
Percent of Students with Transfer-in Credit: 63%
Special Adult Programs: Yes

HOW DOES IT COMPARE?
College Experience: ★★★★
Market Response: ★★
Chance of Getting Out: ★★★★
Chance of Getting In: ★★★
Career Development Potential: ★★★★
Total Cost: High Tuition
Shorter than Average Time to Graduation

MOST POPULAR AREAS OF STUDY
Major Clusters: Quantitative, Analytical/Computational
Most Popular Majors: Business Management 32%, Health Professions 25%, Education 22%

UNIQUE FEATURES
— Gwynedd-Mercy now offers baccalaureate and associate degrees in over 30 majors and five Master of Science programs in Nursing and Education on a full or part-time basis.

— Center for Lifelong Learning offers degree completion accelerated programs in business administration and nursing.

Holy Family Colleges

Grant & Frankford Avenues
Philadelphia, PA 19114
www.hfc.edu, (215) 637-7700

COLLEGE PROFILE
Tuition 2002-2003: $6,995
Average Freshman Institutional Aid Award: $2,712
Percent of Students who Receive Freshman Institutional Aid Award: 89%
Average Student Loan: $2,541
Undergraduate Enrollment - Fall 2001: 1,794
Average Class Size: 12
Demographics of Student Body: African-American 3%, Asian 3%, Caucasian 91%, Hispanic 2%
Percent of Students with Transfer-in Credit: 40%
Special Adult Programs: Yes

HOW DOES IT COMPARE?
College Experience: ★★
Market Response: ★
Chance of Getting Out: ★★★★
Chance of Getting In: ★★★★★
Career Development Potential: ★★
Total Cost: Low Tuition
Shorter than Average Time to Graduation

MOST POPULAR AREAS OF STUDY
Major Clusters: Social Sciences, Quantitative
Most Popular Majors: Education 35%, Business Management 19%, Health Professions 11%

UNIQUE FEATURES
— Holy Family College's Accelerated Degree Program offers a Bachelor of Science degree in Business Administration with concentrations in E-Commerce, Marketing, Human Resource Management, Administration, and Project Management, and a Bachelor of Science degree in Information Systems Management.

— The Accelerated Degree Program also offers a Bachelor of Science degree in Nursing (RN to BSN) and Special Topics courses to fulfill Act 48 requirements through an innovative program designed specifically for working adults.

Mercyhurst College
501 E. 38th Street
Erie, PA 16546
www.mercyhurst.edu, (814) 824-2000

COLLEGE PROFILE
Tuition 2002-2003: $13,940
Average Freshman Institutional Aid Award: $3,089
Percent of Students who Receive Freshman Institutional Aid Award: 88%
Average Student Loan: $3,384
Undergraduate Enrollment - Fall 2001: 3,022
Average Class Size: 20
Demographics of Student Body: African-American 4%, Caucasian 84%, Hispanic 1%
Percent of Students with Transfer-in Credit: 20%
Special Adult Programs: Yes

HOW DOES IT COMPARE?
College Experience: ★★★
Market Response: ★★★
Chance of Getting Out: ★★★
Chance of Getting In: ★
Career Development Potential: ★★★★
Total Cost: High Tuition
Shorter than Average Time to Graduation

MOST POPULAR AREAS OF STUDY
Major Clusters: Analytical/Computational, Social Sciences
Most Popular Majors: Business Management 28%, Education 17%, Social Sciences 12%

UNIQUE FEATURES

— Mercyhurst has the only two-year associate degree program in nursing in the region. The program enrolled its first class at Mercyhurst North East fall 1999. The college has enjoyed a 100 percent placement rate for the two classes of nurses who have completed their studies at Mercyhurst North East.

— In 1992, Mercyhurst began the only four-year, non-government-sponsored intelligence program in the world that trains young men and women for entry-level positions in intelligence, law enforcement, national and corporate security. The Research/Intelligence Analyst program now attracts more than 70 students to Mercyhurst each year.

Saint Joseph University

5600 City Avenue
Philadelphia, PA 19131
www.sju.edu, (610) 660-1000

COLLEGE PROFILE
Tuition 2002-2003: $22,610
Average Freshman Institutional Aid Award: $7,561
Percent of Students who Receive Freshman Institutional Aid Award: 89%
Average Student Loan: $2,773
Undergraduate Enrollment - Fall 2001: 4,517
Average Class Size: 20
Demographics of Student Body: African-American 7%, Asian 2%, Caucasian 82%, Hispanic 2%
Percent of Students with Transfer-in Credit: 95%
Special Adult Programs: Yes

HOW DOES IT COMPARE?
College Experience: ★★★★
Market Response: ★★★★
Chance of Getting Out: ★★★
Chance of Getting In: ★
Career Development Potential: ★★★
Total Cost: High Tuition
Shorter than Average Time to Graduation

MOST POPULAR AREAS OF STUDY
Major Clusters: Analytical/Computational, Social Sciences
Most Popular Majors: Business Management 30%, Social Sciences 14%, Education 12%

UNIQUE FEATURES
— The College's newest facility, The Carol Autorino Center for the Arts and Humanities, houses a 350-seat auditorium, five art galleries to showcase the College's extensive fine arts collections, classrooms, faculty offices and more.

— The campus is easily accessible and offers ample parking, residence halls, dining facilities, the Pope Pius XII Library with over 133,700 volumes and online resources, The O'Connell Athletic Center, and a state-of-the-art Information Technology Network Center.

Temple University
1801 North Broad Street
Philadelphia, PA 19122
www.temple.edu, (215) 204-7000

COLLEGE PROFILE
Tuition 2002-2003: $8,062
Average Freshman Institutional Aid Award: $1,458
Percent of Students who Receive Freshman Institutional Aid Award: 50%
Average Student Loan: $1,759
Undergraduate Enrollment - Fall 2001: 18,394
Average Class Size: 24
Demographics of Student Body: African-American 24%, Asian 8%, Caucasian 53%, Hispanic 3%
Percent of Students with Transfer-in Credit: 49%
Special Adult Programs: Yes

HOW DOES IT COMPARE?
College Experience: ★★★★
Market Response: ★★★★
Chance of Getting Out: ★★★★
Chance of Getting In: ★★★
Career Development Potential: ★★★
Total Cost: Average Tuition
Longer than Average Time to Graduation

MOST POPULAR AREAS OF STUDY
Major Clusters: Analytical/Computational, Social Sciences
Most Popular Majors: Business Management 19%, Education 15%, Communications 10%

UNIQUE FEATURES
— Temple is the 39th largest university in the United States. It also is the largest provider of professional education (law, dentistry, medicine, and podiatric medicine) in the country.

— Through its 16 schools and colleges, Temple University offers degree programs in 9 associate degree areas, 127 bachelors degree areas, 132 masters degree areas, 61 doctoral degree areas, and 6 first professional degree areas.

University of Pittsburgh — Johnstown

450 Schoolhouse Road
Johnstown, PA 15904
(814) 269-7000

COLLEGE PROFILE
Tuition 2002-2003: $3,934
Average Freshman Institutional Aid Award: $2,538
Percent of Students who Receive Freshman Institutional Aid Award: 16%
Average Student Loan: $3,305
Undergraduate Enrollment - Fall 2001: 3,031
Average Class Size: 25-35
Demographics of Student Body: African-American 1%, Asian 1%, Caucasian 98%
Percent of Students with Transfer-in Credit: 14%
Special Adult Programs: Yes

HOW DOES IT COMPARE?
College Experience:	★★★
Market Response:	★
Chance of Getting Out:	★★★
Chance of Getting In:	★★★
Career Development Potential:	★★★
Total Cost:	Low Tuition
	Average Time to Graduation

MOST POPULAR AREAS OF STUDY
Major Clusters: Analytical/Computational, Social Sciences
Most Popular Majors: Education 22%, Business Management 21%, Social Sciences 11%

UNIQUE FEATURES

— Pitt-Johnstown is a four-year degree-granting fully accredited, coeducational, residential undergraduate college of the University of Pittsburgh. With 2,700 well-qualified full-time students and a beautiful suburban campus, Pitt-Johnstown combines the strong academic reputation and outstanding resources of a major research university with the personal appeal of a smaller college.

— Internships, undergraduate research, independent study, academic advising, career counseling, resume workshops, career placement services, and a computerized job-referral system.

Bryant College
1150 Douglas Pike
Smithfield, RI 02917
www.bryant.edu, (401) 232-6000

COLLEGE PROFILE
Tuition 2002-2003: $20,988
Average Freshman Institutional Aid Award: $6,434
Percent of Students who Receive Freshman Institutional Aid Award: 88%
Average Student Loan: $3,579
Undergraduate Enrollment - Fall 2001: 2,699
Average Class Size: 28
Demographics of Student Body: African-American 3%, Asian 2%, Caucasian 83%, Hispanic 3%
Percent of Students with Transfer-in Credit: 14%
Special Adult Programs: Yes

HOW DOES IT COMPARE?
College Experience: ★★★★
Market Response: ★★★★
Chance of Getting Out: ★★★
Chance of Getting In: ★
Career Development Potential: ★★★★
Total Cost: High Tuition
Shorter than Average Time to Graduation

MOST POPULAR AREAS OF STUDY
Major Clusters: Applied Quantitative, Analytical/Computational
Most Popular Majors: Business Management 78%, Computer Information Sciences 21%, English Language and Literature 1%

UNIQUE FEATURES
— Small class sizes, personal attention, and academic programs designed to help develop leadership, communication, decision-making, and social interaction skills make Bryant an environment for intellectual and personal growth.

— Bryant's long tradition of excellence in business and liberal studies in a student-centered environment is enhanced by three new majors in applied psychology, communication, and information technology. The academic programs are complemented by providing all freshman with an IBM laptop and software, which is updated in two years with an option to purchase upon graduation.

Rhode Island College
600 Mount Pleasant Avenue
Providence, RI 02908
www.ric.edu, (401) 456-8000

COLLEGE PROFILE
Tuition 2002-2003: $3,521
Average Freshman Institutional Aid Award: $2,888
Percent of Students who Receive Freshman Institutional Aid Award: 27%
Average Student Loan: $2,787
Undergraduate Enrollment - Fall 2001: 7,060
Average Class Size: 24
Demographics of Student Body: African-American 4%, Asian 2.4%, Caucasian 88.2%, Native American 3%
Percent of Students with Transfer-in Credit: 40%
Special Adult Programs: Yes

HOW DOES IT COMPARE?
College Experience: ★★★
Market Response: ★★★
Chance of Getting Out: ★★★
Chance of Getting In: ★★★★★
Career Development Potential: ★★★★
Total Cost: Low Tuition
Longer than Average Time to Graduation

MOST POPULAR AREAS OF STUDY
Major Clusters: Social Sciences
Most Popular Majors: Education 31%, Health Professions 13%, Psychology 13%

UNIQUE FEATURES
— The first institution of higher education in Rhode Island to provide to its students the use, at no additional charge, of some of the latest and most popular Microsoft operating systems and software applications. The installation and use of these programs is permitted on home computers of the users as well as on campus-based computers.

— Performance Based Admission (PBA) leads to Bachelors degrees for slightly older, non-traditional adult students.

— OUTREACH grant program assists underemployed or dislocated workers who need to advance the skills that will enable them to enter or advance in the workplace

Allen University
1530 Harden Street
Columbia, SC 29204
(803) 254-4165

COLLEGE PROFILE
Tuition 2002-2003: $4,650
Average Freshman Institutional Aid Award: $1,900
Percent of Students who Receive Freshman Institutional Aid Award: 25%
Average Student Loan: $2,000
Undergraduate Enrollment - Fall 2001: 466
Average Class Size: 20
Demographics of Student Body: African-American 97%, Asian 3%
Percent of Students with Transfer-in Credit: 10%
Special Adult Programs: Yes

HOW DOES IT COMPARE?
College Experience: ★★★
Market Response: ★
Chance of Getting Out: ★★★★
Chance of Getting In: ★★★★
Career Development Potential: ★★★★★
Total Cost: Low Tuition
Shorter than Average Time to Graduation

MOST POPULAR AREAS OF STUDY
Major Clusters: Analytical/Computational, Social Sciences
Most Popular Majors: Social Sciences 22%, Liberal Arts 22%
Education 17%

UNIQUE FEATURES
—The University is strategically located in the heart of Columbia, the state capitol, which allows students to take advantage of living in the social and cultural center of the Midlands.

—The University offers academic remediation for entering students, adult/continuing education programs, honors programs, internships, part-time degree program, study abroad, and summer session for credit.

Charleston Southern University

9200 University Blvd.
Charleston, SC 29423
www.csuniv.edu, (843) 863-7000

COLLEGE PROFILE
Tuition 2002-2003: $13,482
Average Freshman Institutional Aid Award: $3,952
Percent of Students who Receive Freshman Institutional Aid Award: 98%
Average Student Loan: $4,920
Undergraduate Enrollment - Fall 2001: 2,543
Average Class Size: 21
Demographics of Student Body: African-American 27%, Asian 1%, Caucasian 47%, Hispanic 5%, Other 18%
Percent of Students with Transfer-in Credit: 53%
Special Adult Programs: Yes

HOW DOES IT COMPARE?
College Experience: ★★★★
Market Response: ★★★
Chance of Getting Out: ★★
Chance of Getting In: ★★★★
Career Development Potential: ★★★★
Total Cost: High Tuition
                     Average Time to Graduation

MOST POPULAR AREAS OF STUDY
Major Clusters: Analytical/Computational, Social Sciences
Most Popular Majors: Business Management 21%, Education 14%, Social Sciences 9%

UNIQUE FEATURES

— The University awards associate's, bachelor's, and master's degrees. Students can choose from more than 30 undergraduate majors and five graduate programs. Each degree program is combined with a comprehensive liberal arts foundation, which is designed to develop problem-solving and communication skills.

— Charleston Southern University's Evening College is the answer to beginning or completing a degree. Whether students wish to enroll full-time or part-time, they may use the school's accelerated course schedule or regular evening college schedule.

Coastal Carolina University
PO Box 261954
Conway, SC 29526
www.coastal.edu, (843) 347-3161

COLLEGE PROFILE
Tuition 2002-2003: $4,350
Average Freshman Institutional Aid Award: $5,401
Percent of Students who Receive Freshman Institutional Aid Award: 23%
Average Student Loan: $3,294
Undergraduate Enrollment - Fall 2001: 4,771
Average Class Size: 19
Demographics of Student Body: African-American 8%, Asian 1%, Caucasian 86%, Hispanic 1%, Other 4%
Percent of Students with Transfer-in Credit: 33%
Special Adult Programs: Yes

HOW DOES IT COMPARE?
College Experience: ★★★
Market Response: ★★
Chance of Getting Out: ★★
Chance of Getting In: ★★★★
Career Development Potential: ★★★★
Total Cost: Low Tuition
Longer than Average Time to Graduation

MOST POPULAR AREAS OF STUDY
Major Clusters: Analytical/Computational, Social Sciences
Most Popular Majors: Marine Science 11%, Marketing 11%, Business Management 10%,

UNIQUE FEATURES
— New degree programs in Middle Grades Education, Music, Philosophy, Spanish, and Special Education are approved.

— A major construction boom increased campus space in 2001 by 30 percent and was highlighted by the opening and formal dedication of the Thomas W. and Robin W. Edwards College of Humanities and Fine Arts, which is the largest building on campus.

Coker College

200 E. College Avenue
Hartsville, SC 29550
www.coker.edu, (843) 383-8000

COLLEGE PROFILE
Tuition 2002-2003: $15,072
Average Freshman Institutional Aid Award: $5,805
Percent of Students who Receive Freshman Institutional Aid Award: 88%
Average Student Loan: $5,530
Undergraduate Enrollment - Fall 2001: 1,068
Average Class Size: 12
Demographics of Student Body: Caucasian 70%, African-American 29%, Hispanic 1%
Percent of Students with Transfer-in Credit: 25%
Special Adult Programs: Yes

HOW DOES IT COMPARE?
College Experience: ★★
Market Response: ★★★
Chance of Getting Out: ★★★
Chance of Getting In: ★★
Career Development Potential: ★★
Total Cost: High Tuition
                Shorter than Average Time to Graduation

MOST POPULAR AREAS OF STUDY
Major Clusters: Analytical/Computational, Social Sciences
Most Popular Majors: Business Management 19%, Biological Sciences 8%, Psychology 7%

UNIQUE FEATURES
— Evening and extended studies program offers adult degree program at night. Many classes use a highly interactive learning style called the "round table."

— While keeping costs down, Coker awards more than $2.9 million a year in institutional financial assistance, in addition to state and federal aid. More than 90% of Coker's students receive financial aid.

College of Charleston

66 George Street
Charleston, SC 29424
www.cofc.edu, (843) 953-5670

COLLEGE PROFILE
Tuition 2002-2003: $4,556
Average Freshman Institutional Aid Award: $2,182
Percent of Students who Receive Freshman Institutional Aid Award: 25%
Average Student Loan: $3,294
Undergraduate Enrollment - Fall 2001: 9,934
Average Class Size: 22
Demographics of Student Body: African-American 9%, Asian 1%, Caucasian 85%, Hispanic 1%
Percent of Students with Transfer-in Credit: 38%
Special Adult Programs: Yes

HOW DOES IT COMPARE?
College Experience: ★★★
Market Response: ★★★★
Chance of Getting Out: ★★★★
Chance of Getting In: ★★★
Career Development Potential: ★★
Total Cost: Low Tuition
Average Time to Graduation

MOST POPULAR AREAS OF STUDY
Major Clusters: Analytical/Computational, Social Sciences
Most Popular Majors: Business Management 19%, Education 14%, Communications 13%

UNIQUE FEATURES
— The Spring 2002 semester saw the debut of three new computer science distance education courses. Video and audio links enabled students at College of Charleston- North in North Charleston to be part of classes taught in specially equipped classrooms at the downtown campus.

— The College of Charleston's undergraduate research program reaped numerous awards at the South Carolina Academy of Science 75th Annual Meeting held recently at the University of South Carolina- Aiken. (7/3/2002)

— 3 week-Maymester offers travel courses to France and Spain as well as other international locations with special courses affiliated with the International Arts Festival.

Columbia College

1301 Columbia College Drive
Columbia, SC 29203
www.colacoll.edu, (803) 786-3012

COLLEGE PROFILE
Tuition 2002-2003: $16,270
Average Freshman Institutional Aid Award: $5,325
Percent of Students who Receive Freshman Institutional Aid Award: 97%
Average Student Loan: $4,435
Undergraduate Enrollment - Fall 2001: 1,206
Average Class Size: 20
Demographics of Student Body: African-American 42%, Caucasian 57%, Hispanic 1%
Percent of Students with Transfer-in Credit: 59%
Special Adult Programs: Yes

HOW DOES IT COMPARE?
College Experience: ★★★★
Market Response: ★★★
Chance of Getting Out: ★★★
Chance of Getting In: ★★★★
Career Development Potential: ★★★
Total Cost: High Tuition
                     Shorter than Average Time to Graduation

MOST POPULAR AREAS OF STUDY
Major Clusters: Quantitative, Analytical/Computational
Most Popular Majors: Education 22%, Public Administration 14%, Business Administration 14%

UNIQUE FEATURES
— Students living in college residence halls have free access to Cougar ResNet, a high-speed Internet service. All students, whether they live on or off campus, can use the large, general-purpose Student Computing Centers, departmental computing labs, and residence hall computing labs.

— The Leadership Institute trains women of all ages to assume positions of leadership within their professions and communities.

—The Premedical Program is designed to guide students in their preparation for admission to medical, dental, or veterinary schools, as well as other health related graduate professional programs.

Get In. Get Out. Get a Job. // 187

Converse College
580 East Main
Spartanburg, SC 29302
www.converse.edu, (864) 596-9040

COLLEGE PROFILE
Tuition 2002-2003: $16,580
Average Freshman Institutional Aid Award: $8,505
Percent of Students who Receive Freshman Institutional Aid Award: 94%
Average Student Loan: $3,601
Undergraduate Enrollment - Fall 2001: 623
Average Class Size: 20
Demographics of Student Body: African-American 10%, Asian 1%, Caucasian 79%, Hispanic 2%
Percent of Students with Transfer-in Credit: 5%
Special Adult Programs: Yes

HOW DOES IT COMPARE?
College Experience: ★★★
Market Response: ★★★
Chance of Getting Out: ★★
Chance of Getting In: ★★
Career Development Potential: ★★★★
Total Cost: High Tuition
Shorter than Average Time to Graduation

MOST POPULAR AREAS OF STUDY
Major Clusters: Social Sciences, Fine Arts
Most Popular Majors: Education 23%, Visual & Performing Arts 18%, Business Management 17%

UNIQUE FEATURES
— The Campaign for Converse: Building for the Future surpassed its $75 million goal one year ahead of the original June 30, 2003 completion date.

— Enhancement plans included three new constructions: The Sally Abney Rose Physical Activity Complex (now complete), the "Nita" Milliken Addition to Milliken Fine Arts Building (also complete), and Phifer Science and Technology Building (scheduled to begin next year). Also included are major renovations to many existing campus buildings, including residence halls and Montgomery Student Center.

Francis Marion University
PO Box 100547
Florence, SC 29501
www.fmarion.edu, (843) 661-1362

COLLEGE PROFILE
Tuition 2002-2003: $4,190
Average Freshman Institutional Aid Award: $2,333
Percent of Students who Receive Freshman Institutional Aid Award: 47%
Average Student Loan: $3,593
Undergraduate Enrollment - Fall 2001: 2,822
Average Class Size: 20
Demographics of Student Body: African-American 31.3%, Asian 1%, Caucasian 63%, Hispanic 1%
Percent of Students with Transfer-in Credit: 23%
Special Adult Programs: Yes

HOW DOES IT COMPARE?
College Experience: ★★
Market Response: ★★
Chance of Getting Out: ★★
Chance of Getting In: ★★★★★
Career Development Potential: ★
Total Cost: Low Tuition
Longer than Average Time to Graduation

MOST POPULAR AREAS OF STUDY
Major Clusters: Quantitative, Analytical/Computational
Most Popular Majors: Business Management 32%, Health Professions 25%, Education 22%

UNIQUE FEATURES
— FMU has the look and feel of a small, liberal arts college with all the benefits of a state-supported comprehensive university. The school is small enough to afford students personalized attention from faculty and staff, and large enough to let you expand your horizons.

— FMU also provides numerous services to the community, region and public at large. Additionally, the University offers programs and services in continuing education, technical and professional assistance, industrial and economic development and artistic and cultural enrichment.

Southern Wesleyan University
907 Wesleyan Drive
Central, SC 29630
www.swu.edu, (864) 639-2453

COLLEGE PROFILE
Tuition 2002-2003: $12,400
Average Freshman Institutional Aid Award: $2,438
Percent of Students who Receive Freshman Institutional Aid Award: 61%
Average Student Loan: $3,393
Undergraduate Enrollment - Fall 2001: 1,996
Average Class Size: 18
Demographics of Student Body: African-American 26%,
 Caucasian 69%, Hispanic 1%
Percent of Students with Transfer-in Credit: 70%
Special Adult Programs: Yes

HOW DOES IT COMPARE?
College Experience: ★★
Market Response: ★★
Chance of Getting Out: ★★★
Chance of Getting In: ★★★★★
Career Development Potential: ★
Total Cost: Average Tuition
                   Average Time to Graduation

MOST POPULAR AREAS OF STUDY
Major Clusters: Analytical/Computational, Social Sciences
Most Popular Majors: Business 74%, Education 11%,
                       Philosophy 6%

UNIQUE FEATURES
— Southern Wesleyan University is proud to announce a new program available for the Fall 2002 semester. The new Bachelor of Science in e-Commerce Management is slated to begin in August.

— Founded in 1986, the Leadership Education for Adult Professionals (LEAP) program provides defined, accelerated learning systems for today's working adults to get ahead. Efficient curriculum plans fit today's busy lifestyles. Streamlined registration procedures and convenient class scheduling are the hallmarks of the LEAP program's service ethic, together with accommodating financial support. Through LEAP mature professionals can further their education and build rewarding futures.

University of South Carolina — Aiken

471 University Parkway
Aiken, SC 29801
www.usca.edu, (803) 648-6851

COLLEGE PROFILE
Tuition 2002-2003: $2,137
Average Freshman Institutional Aid Award: $1,873
Percent of Students who Receive Freshman Institutional Aid Award: 26%
Average Student Loan: $1,635
Undergraduate Enrollment - Fall 2001: 3,100
Average Class Size: 18
Demographics of Student Body: African American 20%, Asian 1%, Caucasian 76%, Hispanic 1%
Percent of Students with Transfer-in Credit: 30%
Special Adult Programs: Yes

HOW DOES IT COMPARE?
College Experience: ★★★★
Market Response: ★★★
Chance of Getting Out: ★★★
Chance of Getting In: ★★★★
Career Development Potential: ★★
Total Cost: Low Tuition
Longer than Average Time to Graduation

MOST POPULAR AREAS OF STUDY
Major Clusters: Analytical/Computational, Social Sciences
Most Popular Majors: Business Management 30%, Education 17%, Health Professions 9%

UNIQUE FEATURES
— Academy of Lifelong Learning is an extensive co-educational program for mature adults offering: intellectual stimulation and social interaction through lectures, short courses, field trips, discussion groups, and community information seminars.

— As one of the fastest growing institutions in the USC system, USC Aiken has consistently recruited traditional and non-traditional students, i.e. those who are married, senior citizens and persons who are returning to school after an extended absence.

University of South Carolina — Spartanburg
800 University Way
Spartanburg, SC 29303
www.uscs.edu, (864) 503-5000

COLLEGE PROFILE
Tuition 2002-2003: $4,631
Average Freshman Institutional Aid Award: $2,907
Percent of Students who Receive Freshman Institutional Aid Award: 73%
Average Student Loan: $1,584
Undergraduate Enrollment - Fall 2001: 3,899
Average Class Size: 20
Demographics of Student Body: African-American 24%, Asian 2%, Hispanic 2%, Caucasian 68%
Percent of Students with Transfer-in Credit: 41%
Special Adult Programs: Yes

HOW DOES IT COMPARE?
College Experience: ★★
Market Response: ★★
Chance of Getting Out: ★★
Chance of Getting In: ★★★★
Career Development Potential: ★★★
Total Cost: Low Tuition
Longer than Average Time to Graduation

MOST POPULAR AREAS OF STUDY
Major Clusters: Analytical/Computational, Social Sciences
Most Popular Majors: Business Management 17%, Education 8%, Health Professions 8%

UNIQUE FEATURES
— Students at USCS have countless opportunities to participate in campus activities and to assume leadership roles in a variety of organizations.

— Students can also take advantage of the many student services offered to complement the academic program—internship opportunities (regional, national and international), the Women's Resource Center, special programs for minority and international students and the Career Services Center are just a few of the many services offered.

Northern State University
1200 South Jay Street
Aberdeen, SD 57401
www.northern.edu, (800) 678-5330

COLLEGE PROFILE
Tuition 2002-2003: $3,874
Average Freshman Institutional Aid Award: $1,030
Percent of Students who Receive Freshman Institutional Aid Award: 52%
Average Student Loan: $3,236
Undergraduate Enrollment - Fall 2001: 2,562
Average Class Size: 17
Demographics of Student Body: African-American 2%, Asian 1%, Caucasian 86%, Hispanic 1%, Native American 2%
Percent of Students with Transfer-in Credit: 10%
Special Adult Programs: Yes

HOW DOES IT COMPARE?
College Experience: ★★
Market Response: ★★
Chance of Getting Out: ★★
Chance of Getting In: ★★★★★
Career Development Potential: ★★
Total Cost: Low Tuition
Average Time to Graduation

MOST POPULAR AREAS OF STUDY
Major Clusters: Analytical/Computational, Social Sciences
Most Popular Majors: Business Management 31%, Education 28%, Social Sciences 10%

UNIQUE FEATURES
— Two-year programs are provided in specialized areas; they lead to associate of arts and associate of science degrees. Northern offers the only international business program in South Dakota.

— The E-Learning Center works to create distant learning links between NSU and the State's public school system.

Christian Brothers University

650 East Parkway South
Memphis, TN 38104
www.cbu.edu, (901) 321-3000

COLLEGE PROFILE

Tuition 2002-2003: $15,790
Average Freshman Institutional Aid Award: $6,902
Percent of Students who Receive Freshman Institutional Aid Award: 89%
Average Student Loan: $4,056
Undergraduate Enrollment - Fall 2001: 1,584
Average Class Size: 13
Demographics of Student Body: African-American 325, Asian 3%,
 Caucasian 56%, Hispanic 1%
Percent of Students with Transfer-in Credit: 5%
Special Adult Programs: Yes

HOW DOES IT COMPARE?

College Experience: ★★★★
Market Response: ★★★
Chance of Getting Out: ★★
Chance of Getting In: ★★★
Career Development Potential: ★★★★
Total Cost: High Tuition
                    Average Time to Graduation

MOST POPULAR AREAS OF STUDY

Major Clusters: Applied Quantitative, Analytical/Computational
Most Popular Majors: Business Management 49%, Engineering 15%,
                        Psychology 11%

UNIQUE FEATURES

— CBU was the first private institution in Memphis to integrate.

— Evening Program is for working adults pursuing an undergraduate education in business, applied psychology, or teacher education.

Crichton College

6655 Winchester Street
Memphis, TN 38175
www.crichton.edu, (901) 367-9800

COLLEGE PROFILE
Tuition 2002-2003: $9,520
Average Freshman Institutional Aid Award: $1,962
Percent of Students who Receive Freshman Institutional Aid Award: 54%
Average Student Loan: $5,168
Undergraduate Enrollment - Fall 2001: 963
Average Class Size: 20
Demographics of Student Body: African-American 49%, Caucasian 44%
Percent of Students with Transfer-in Credit: 65%
Special Adult Programs: Yes

HOW DOES IT COMPARE?
College Experience: ★★
Market Response: ★★
Chance of Getting Out: ★★
Chance of Getting In: ★★★★★
Career Development Potential: ★★
Total Cost: Average Tuition
                    Longer than Average Time to Graduation

MOST POPULAR AREAS OF STUDY
Major Clusters: Analytical/Computational, Social Sciences
Most Popular Majors: Business Management 69%, Education 18%,
                        Theological Studies 6%

UNIQUE FEATURES
Saint Joseph Hospital, one of the oldest hospitals in Nebraska, and the Creighton University Health Sciences Division officially became linked today under their new name: Creighton University Medical Center. The new name clarifies the position of Saint Joseph Hospital as the teaching hospital of Creighton University and reinforces the institution's position as one of the premier academic medical centers in the region.

Fisk University

1000 17th Avenue North
Nashville, TN 37203
www.fisk.edu, (615) 329-8500

COLLEGE PROFILE
Tuition 2002-2003: $10,100
Average Freshman Institutional Aid Award: $3,200
Percent of Students who Receive Freshman Institutional Aid Award: 38%
Average Student Loan: $2,625
Undergraduate Enrollment - Fall 2001: 786
Average Class Size: 17
Demographics of Student Body: African-American 94%, Other 6%
Percent of Students with Transfer-in Credit: 18%
Special Adult Programs: n/a

HOW DOES IT COMPARE?
College Experience: ★★★
Market Response: ★★★★
Chance of Getting Out: ★★★★
Chance of Getting In: ★★★★★
Career Development Potential: ★★
Total Cost: Average Tuition
                    Shorter than Average Time to Graduation

MOST POPULAR AREAS OF STUDY
Major Clusters: Social Sciences, Analytical/Computational
Most Popular Majors: Biological Sciences 18%, Psychology 16%,
                     Political Sciences 5%

UNIQUE FEATURES
— In proportion to enrollment, a greater percentage of Fisk graduates achieve the Ph.D. degree than the minority graduates of any other U.S. college or university.

— McNaik Scholar/Lead Program: Geared toward first generation minority college students. The Program prepares them to pursue doctoral degrees and is sponsored by the U.S. Department of Education.

LeMoyne-Owen College
807 Walker Avenue
Memphis, TN 38126
www.lemoyne-owen.edu, (901) 774-9090

COLLEGE PROFILE
Tuition 2002-2003: $8,250
Average Freshman Institutional Aid Award: $5,549
Percent of Students who Receive Freshman Institutional Aid Award: 24%
Average Student Loan: $5,067
Undergraduate Enrollment - Fall 2001: 734
Average Class Size: 20
Demographics of Student Body: African-American 95%, Asian 1%, Other 4%
Percent of Students with Transfer-in Credit: 50%
Special Adult Programs: Yes

HOW DOES IT COMPARE?
College Experience: ★★
Market Response: ★
Chance of Getting Out: ★★★
Chance of Getting In: ★★★★★
Career Development Potential: ★★
Total Cost: Average Tuition
                        Longer than Average Time to Graduation

MOST POPULAR AREAS OF STUDY
Major Clusters: Analytical/Computational, Social Sciences
Most Popular Majors: Business Management 41%, Education 25%, Social Sciences 14%

UNIQUE FEATURES
The Evening and Weekend Program offers non-traditional and working students an opportunity to pursue a College education through evening and weekend course work. A variety of Core general education and elective courses is offered. Students can complete baccalaureate degrees in Business Administration (but not with the Accounting concentration), Education, Social Work or Criminal Justice through courses offered at night or on weekends.

Tennessee State University

3500 John A. Merrit Blvd.
Nashville, TN 37209
www.tnstate.edu, (615) 963-5111

COLLEGE PROFILE
Tuition 2002-2003: $3,008
Average Freshman Institutional Aid Award: $3,682
Percent of Students who Receive Freshman Institutional Aid Award: 21%
Average Student Loan: $2,814
Undergraduate Enrollment - Fall 2001: 7,060
Average Class Size: 25
Demographics of Student Body: African-American 76%, Asian 2%, Caucasian 21%, Hispanic 1%
Percent of Students with Transfer-in Credit: 43%
Special Adult Programs: Yes

HOW DOES IT COMPARE?
College Experience: ★★
Market Response: ★★★
Chance of Getting Out: ★★★
Chance of Getting In: ★★★
Career Development Potential: ★★★
Total Cost: Low Tuition
Average Time to Graduation

MOST POPULAR AREAS OF STUDY
Major Clusters: Quantitative, Verbal
Most Popular Majors: Liberal Arts 17%, Business Management 16%, Health Professions 14%

UNIQUE FEATURES
— The three-story Martha M. Brown/Lois H. Daniel Library has an impressive collection of resources supporting the college curriculum as well as the research needs of those in the surrounding areas.

— Alma Mater of Oprah Winfrey.

Trevecca Nazarene College
333 Murfreesboro Road
Nashville, TN 37210
www.trevecca.edu, (615) 248-1200

COLLEGE PROFILE
Tuition 2002-2003: $11,390
Average Freshman Institutional Aid Award: $4,231
Percent of Students who Receive Freshman Institutional Aid Award: 90%
Average Student Loan: $4,176
Undergraduate Enrollment - Fall 2001: 1,159
Average Class Size: 18
Demographics of Student Body: African-American 10%, Asian 1%, Caucasian 81%, Hispanic 2%,
Percent of Students with Transfer-in Credit: n/a
Special Adult Programs: Yes

HOW DOES IT COMPARE?
College Experience: ★★★
Market Response: ★★
Chance of Getting Out: ★★
Chance of Getting In: ★★★★★
Career Development Potential: ★★★★
Total Cost: Average Tuition
                 Average Time to Graduation

MOST POPULAR AREAS OF STUDY
Major Clusters: Analytical/Computational, Social Sciences
Most Popular Majors: Business Management 68%, Education 7%, Philosophy 7%

UNIQUE FEATURES
— Trevecca's School of Religion is accepting applications for admission into the new D.A. in Religion Program. This newest addition to Trevecca's academic offerings is designed for teachers, pastors, denominational leaders, missionaries who desire a terminal degree.

— MBA and MSM degrees: An alternative to the traditional MBA degree for professional adults. Classes are offered at night and on weekends.

Dallas Baptist University

3000 Mountain Creek Parkway
Dallas, TX 75211
www.dbu.edu, (214) 333-7100

COLLEGE PROFILE

Tuition 2002-2003: $10,350
Average Freshman Institutional Aid Award: $4,554
Percent of Students who Receive Freshman Institutional Aid Award: 74%
Average Student Loan: $2,919
Undergraduate Enrollment - Fall 2001: 3,340
Average Class Size: 16
Demographics of Student Body: African-American 21%, Asian 2%,
    Caucasian 54%, Hispanic 7%, Native American 2%,
Percent of Students with Transfer-in Credit: 58%
Special Adult Programs: Yes

HOW DOES IT COMPARE?

College Experience: ★★★
Market Response: ★★★
Chance of Getting Out: ★★
Chance of Getting In: ★★★★★
Career Development Potential: ★★★
Total Cost: Average Tuition
Shorter than Average Time to Graduation

MOST POPULAR AREAS OF STUDY

Major Clusters: Analytical/Computational, Verbal
Most Popular Majors: Business Management 44%, Liberal Arts 22%,
Visual and Performing Arts 7%

UNIQUE FEATURES

— College of Adult Education provides a quality educational experience through unique bachelor's degree program; working adults may earn up to 30 hours of college credit through prior learning assessment.

— Online courses are a powerful means of course delivery at DBU! As the University responds to students needs via its virtual university at www.dbu.online.org. Four complete online degree options and an exceptional ecommerce certification program empower learners whose daily schedule makes a commute to campus impossible.

DeVry University
4800 Regent Blvd.
Irving, TX 75063
www.dal.devry.edu, (972) 926-6777

COLLEGE PROFILE
Tuition 2002-2003: $8,740
Average Freshman Institutional Aid Award: $3,595
Percent of Students who Receive Freshman Institutional Aid Award: n/a
Average Student Loan: $5,462
Undergraduate Enrollment - Fall 2001: 3,569
Average Class Size: 20
Demographics of Student Body: African-American 30%, Asian 8%, Caucasian 43%, Hispanic 16%
Percent of Students with Transfer-in Credit: 9%
Special Adult Programs: Yes

HOW DOES IT COMPARE?
College Experience: ★★★
Market Response: ★★★
Chance of Getting Out: ★★
Chance of Getting In: ★★★★★
Career Development Potential: ★★★
Total Cost: Average Tuition
                    Average Time to Graduation

MOST POPULAR AREAS OF STUDY
Major Clusters: Applied Quantitative
Most Popular Majors: Business Management 44%, Computer & Information Sciences 39%, Engineering Technologies 17%

UNIQUE FEATURES
DeVry Outreach Services offers a variety of public service programs dedicated to helping educators, students and parents keep up-to-date on the latest trends on opportunities in business and technology and the skills needed to be successful in these fields.

Houston Baptist University

7502 Fondren Road
Houston, TX 77074
www.hbu.edu, (281) 649-3000

COLLEGE PROFILE
Tuition 2002-2003: $10,500
Average Freshman Institutional Aid Award: $4,256
Percent of Students who Receive Freshman Institutional Aid Award: 79%
Average Student Loan: $6,209
Undergraduate Enrollment - Fall 2001: 1,953
Average Class Size: 20
Demographics of Student Body: African-American 19%, Asian 8%, Caucasian 51%, Hispanic 20%
Percent of Students with Transfer-in Credit: 20%
Special Adult Programs: Yes

HOW DOES IT COMPARE?
College Experience:	★★
Market Response:	★★★★
Chance of Getting Out:	★★★★
Chance of Getting In:	★★★★
Career Development Potential:	★★
Total Cost:	Average Tuition
	Longer than Average Time to Graduation

MOST POPULAR AREAS OF STUDY
Major Clusters: Quantitative, Analytical/Computational
Most Popular Majors: Business Management 32%, Health Professions 25%, Education 22%

UNIQUE FEATURES
— The University prepares its graduates to enter the work force of the twenty-first century, to pursue advanced study, to assume leadership roles, and to be competitive in a global society.

— Enrichment Center conducts Freshman Seminars to help first-year students make the transition to university life easily.

Our Lady of the Lake University of San Antonio

411 SW 24th Street
San Antonio, TX 78207
www.allusa.edu, (210) 434-6711

COLLEGE PROFILE
Tuition 2002-2003: $12,786
Average Freshman Institutional Aid Award: $4,257
Percent of Students who Receive Freshman Institutional Aid Award: 96%
Average Student Loan: $3,810
Undergraduate Enrollment - Fall 2001: 2,233
Average Class Size: 17
Demographics of Student Body: African-American 6%, Asian 1%, Caucasian 22%, Hispanic 63%
Percent of Students with Transfer-in Credit: 18%
Special Adult Programs: Yes

HOW DOES IT COMPARE?
College Experience: ★★★
Market Response: ★
Chance of Getting Out: ★★
Chance of Getting In: ★★★★★
Career Development Potential: ★★★
Total Cost: Average Tuition
Longer than Average Time to Graduation

MOST POPULAR AREAS OF STUDY
Major Clusters: Analytical/Computational, Verbal
Most Popular Majors: Business Management 25%, Psychology 13%, Liberal Arts 10%

UNIQUE FEATURES
OLLU is the first academic institution in Texas to offer an Online Master Technology Teacher (MTT) Program, a Texas certification program. The program is designed to provide comprehensive training for teachers to increase the use of technology in classrooms (from early childhood to secondary).

St. Edward's University
2001 South Congress Avenue
Austin, TX 78704
www.stedwards.edu, (512) 448-8400

COLLEGE PROFILE
Tuition 2002-2003: $13,620
Average Freshman Institutional Aid Award: $4,592
Percent of Students who Receive Freshman Institutional Aid Award: 67%
Average Student Loan: $4,212
Undergraduate Enrollment - Fall 2001: 3,369
Average Class Size: 21
Demographics of Student Body: African-American 6%, Asian 3%, Caucasian 57%, Hispanic 5%
Percent of Students with Transfer-in Credit: 36%
Special Adult Programs: Yes

HOW DOES IT COMPARE?
College Experience: ★★★★
Market Response: ★★★★
Chance of Getting Out: ★★
Chance of Getting In: ★★★★★
Career Development Potential: ★★★★
Total Cost: High Tuition
Average Time to Graduation

MOST POPULAR AREAS OF STUDY
Major Clusters: Analytical/Computational
Most Popular Majors: Communications 9%, Psychology 7%, Business Administration. 6%,

UNIQUE FEATURES
— Special programs offered: double majors, independent study, accelerated program, honors program, pass/fail grading option, internships and distance learning, and a MBA Program for working professionals in the evening and on weekends.

— Study abroad opportunities: Member of International Student Exchange Program (ISEP). Exchange programs abroad in Germany (Koblenz) and Mexico (ITESM).

Texas A&M University — Corpus Christi

6300 Ocean Drive
Corpus Christi, TX 78412
www.tamucc.edu, (361) 825-5700

COLLEGE PROFILE
Tuition 2002-2003: $3,058
Average Freshman Institutional Aid Award: $2,211
Percent of Students who Receive Freshman Institutional Aid Award: 21%
Average Student Loan: $2,822
Undergraduate Enrollment - Fall 2001: 5,329
Average Class Size: 27
Demographics of Student Body: African-American 2%, Asian 2%, Caucasian 55%, Hispanic 39%
Percent of Students with Transfer-in Credit: 65%
Special Adult Programs: n/a

HOW DOES IT COMPARE?
College Experience: ★★★★
Market Response: ★★★
Chance of Getting Out: ★★
Chance of Getting In: ★★★★
Career Development Potential: ★★★
Total Cost: Low Tuition
Longer than Average Time to Graduation

MOST POPULAR AREAS OF STUDY
Major Clusters: Analytical/Computational, Verbal
Most Popular Majors: Business Management 21%, Interdisciplinary Studies 15%, Health Professions 9%

UNIQUE FEATURES
Program offerings in the four academic colleges now include more than 55 undergraduate and graduate degree programs. Additional degree programs are planned and will be offered following state approval.

Texas A&M University — Galveston

200 Sea Wolf Parkway
Galveston, TX 77553
www.tamug.tamu.edu, (409) 740-4400

COLLEGE PROFILE
Tuition 2002-2003: $3,233
Average Freshman Institutional Aid Award: $1,285
Percent of Students who Receive Freshman Institutional Aid Award: 20%
Average Student Loan: $4,065
Undergraduate Enrollment - Fall 2001: 1,356
Average Class Size: 20
Demographics of Student Body: African American 1%, Asian 2%, Caucasian 84%, Hispanic 9%
Percent of Students with Transfer-in Credit: 93%
Special Adult Programs: n/a

HOW DOES IT COMPARE?
College Experience: ★★★
Market Response: ★★★
Chance of Getting Out: ★★★
Chance of Getting In: ★★★
Career Development Potential: ★★
Total Cost:	Low Tuition
	Longer than Average Time to Graduation

MOST POPULAR AREAS OF STUDY
Major Clusters:	Quantitative, Analytical/Computational
Most Popular Majors:	Biological Sciences 38%, Business & Marketing 24%
	Physical Sciences 16%

UNIQUE FEATURES
Texas A&M University at Galveston (TAMUG) is an ocean-oriented campus offering education, research and public service in marine engineering, marine biology, oceanography, business, and marine transportation.

Texas Christian University
2800 S. University Drive
Fort Worth, TX 76129
www.tcu.edu, (817) 257-7000

COLLEGE PROFILE
Tuition 2002-2003: $16,300
Average Freshman Institutional Aid Award: $4,811
Percent of Students who Receive Freshman Institutional Aid Award: 77%
Average Student Loan: $3,392
Undergraduate Enrollment - Fall 2001: 6,885
Average Class Size: 27
Demographics of Student Body: African-American 5%, Asian 2%, Caucasian 78%, Hispanic 6%, Native American 1%
Percent of Students with Transfer-in Credit: 21%
Special Adult Programs: n/a

HOW DOES IT COMPARE?
College Experience: ★★★★★
Market Response: ★
Chance of Getting Out: ★★★★
Chance of Getting In: ★★
Career Development Potential: ★★★
Total Cost: High Tuition
Shorter than Average Time to Graduation

MOST POPULAR AREAS OF STUDY
Major Clusters: Analytical/Computational, Verbal
Most Popular Majors: Business Management 29%, Communications 14%
Health Professions 7%

UNIQUE FEATURES
— With funding from both federal and local agencies, the newly-created Institute for Mathematics, Science, and Technology Education brings together faculty from different disciplines to discover new and innovative ways of teaching and learning quantitative skills and abilities.

— The Journalism Program is one of only ten in U.S. private universities and the only in a five-state area approved by the Accrediting Council on Education in Journalism and Mass Communications

Texas Wesleyan University

1201 Wesleyan
Fort Worth, TX 76105
www.txwesleyan.edu, (817) 531-4444

COLLEGE PROFILE
Tuition 2002-2003: $10,306
Average Freshman Institutional Aid Award: $4,549
Percent of Students who Receive Freshman Institutional Aid Award: 95%
Average Student Loan: $3,743
Undergraduate Enrollment - Fall 2001: 1,714
Average Class Size: 17
Demographics of Student Body: Caucasian 65%, African-American 13%, Hispanic 13%
Percent of Students with Transfer-in Credit: 22%
Special Adult Programs: Yes

HOW DOES IT COMPARE?
College Experience: ★★★
Market Response: ★★★
Chance of Getting Out: ★★
Chance of Getting In: ★★★
Career Development Potential: ★★★
Total Cost: Average Tuition
Average Time to Graduation

MOST POPULAR AREAS OF STUDY
Major Clusters: Analytical/Computational, Social Sciences
Most Popular Majors: Business Management 26%, Education 17%, Psychology 9%

UNIQUE FEATURES
— C.E. Hyde Weekend University Program is designed for adult students who want to earn a degree in business, or select areas of science and humanities. Most of the courses for these degrees are offered on the weekends, and students can complete a degree by attending only on the weekends. They can also take classes during the day if they need to.

— Texas Wesleyan students take part in internships, where they receive academic credit for working off-campus in a business or service organization related to their major areas of study.

University of Houston — Clear Lake

2700 Bay Area Blvd.
Houston, TX 77058
(281) 283-7600

COLLEGE PROFILE
Tuition 2002-2003: $7,328
Average Freshman Institutional Aid Award: n/a
Percent of Students who Receive Freshman Institutional Aid Award: n/a
Average Student Loan: n/a
Undergraduate Enrollment - Fall 2001: 3,850
Average Class Size: 24
Demographics of Student Body: African-American 9%, Asian 8%, Caucasian 64%, Hispanic 12%
Percent of Students with Transfer-in Credit: 100%
Special Adult Programs: Yes

HOW DOES IT COMPARE?
College Experience: ★★★
Market Response: ★
Chance of Getting Out: ★★
Chance of Getting In: ★★★★
Career Development Potential: ★★★★
Total Cost: Low Tuition
                    Average Time to Graduation

MOST POPULAR AREAS OF STUDY
Major Clusters: Analytical/Computational, Verbal
Most Popular Majors: Business Management 31%, Interdisciplinary Studies 18%, Computer Information Sciences 9%

UNIQUE FEATURES
— Offers more than 30 undergraduate degree programs and over 40 graduate degree programs to approximately 7,600 upper-level students enrolled in its four schools—School of Business and Public Administration, School of Education, School of Human Sciences and Humanities, and School of Science and Computer Engineering.

— School of Science and Computer Engineering enjoys a long-standing professional relationship with NASA's Johnson Space Center and its contractors who played a major role in the addition of the master of science in systems engineering degree program.

University of Houston — Downtown
1 Main Street
Houston, TX 77002
www.dt.uh.edu, (713) 221-8000

COLLEGE PROFILE
Tuition 2002-2003: $2,474
Average Freshman Institutional Aid Award: $1,147
Percent of Students who Receive Freshman Institutional Aid Award: 15%
Average Student Loan: $2,603
Undergraduate Enrollment - Fall 2001: 8,932
Average Class Size: 24
Demographics of Student Body: African-American 29%, Asian 11%, Caucasian 25%, Hispanic 32%
Percent of Students with Transfer-in Credit: 59%
Special Adult Programs: Yes

HOW DOES IT COMPARE?
College Experience: ★★★★
Market Response: ★★
Chance of Getting Out: ★★
Chance of Getting In: ★★★★★
Career Development Potential: ★★★
Total Cost: Low Tuition
Average Time to Graduation

MOST POPULAR AREAS OF STUDY
Major Clusters: Analytical/Computational, Verbal
Most Popular Majors: Business Management 47%, Liberal Arts 15%, Protective Services 10%

UNIQUE FEATURES
— At UHD, get state-of-the-art technology, and flexible course options, including classes in The Woodlands, Fort Bend County and Channelview area.

— More than 30 degree programs.

University of Texas — Arlington
701 S. Nedderman Drive
Arlington, TX 76013
www.uta.edu, (817) 272-2222

COLLEGE PROFILE
Tuition 2002-2003: $3,068
Average Freshman Institutional Aid Award: $1,698
Percent of Students who Receive Freshman Institutional Aid Award: 31%
Average Student Loan: $4,827
Undergraduate Enrollment - Fall 2001: 16,330
Average Class Size: 27
Demographics of Student Body: African-American 12%, Asian 10%, Caucasian 56%, Hispanic 11%, Native American 1%
Percent of Students with Transfer-in Credit: 71%
Special Adult Programs: Yes

HOW DOES IT COMPARE?
College Experience: ★★★
Market Response: ★★★
Chance of Getting Out: ★★
Chance of Getting In: ★★★★
Career Development Potential: ★★★
Total Cost: Low Tuition
              Longer than Average Time to Graduation

MOST POPULAR AREAS OF STUDY
Major Clusters: Analytical/Computational, Quantitative
Most Popular Majors: Marketing 31%, Health Professions 10%, Engineering 10%

UNIQUE FEATURES
— Adult Student Seminars offered by the Counseling and Career Development Office.

— Leader in Internet-based education.

— School's location makes it a rich laboratory for student projects, research, internships, and career opportunities with some of the nation's largest and prestigious firms.

University of the Incarnate Word
4301 Broadway
San Antonio, TX 78209
www.uiw.edu, (210) 829-6000

COLLEGE PROFILE
Tuition 2002-2003: $14,000
Average Freshman Institutional Aid Award: $4,344
Percent of Students who Receive Freshman Institutional Aid Award: 68%
Average Student Loan: $5,819
Undergraduate Enrollment - Fall 2001: 3,003
Average Class Size: 20
Demographics of Student Body: African-American 6%, Asian 2%, Caucasian 26%, Hispanic 54%
Percent of Students with Transfer-in Credit: 45%
Special Adult Programs: n/a

HOW DOES IT COMPARE?
College Experience: ★★★
Market Response: ★★★★
Chance of Getting Out: ★★
Chance of Getting In: ★★★
Career Development Potential: ★★★
Total Cost: High Tuition
Longer than Average Time to Graduation

MOST POPULAR AREAS OF STUDY
Major Clusters: Analytical/Computational, Quantitative
Most Popular Majors: Business Management 39%, Liberal Arts 11%, Health Professions 11%

UNIQUE FEATURES
— Incarnate Word High School has been recognized as a 2001-2002 National Blue Ribbon School of Excellence. IWHS is the only Catholic School in Texas to receive the honor, and is one of 172 schools recognized nationally.

— The University of the Incarnate Word hosts free classes in summer and fall which serve as a bridge between high school and college. The classes are geared to students who will be entering UIW immediately after high school as well as those who will be returning to school after extended breaks.

College of Saint Joseph

71 Clement Road
Rutland, VT 05701
www.csj.edu, (802) 773-5900

COLLEGE PROFILE

Tuition 2002-2003: $12,000
Average Freshman Institutional Aid Award: $4,198
Percent of Students who Receive Freshman Institutional Aid Award: 57%
Average Student Loan: $2,462
Undergraduate Enrollment - Fall 2001: 314
Average Class Size: 11
Demographics of Student Body: African-American 3%, Asian 1%, Caucasian 91%, Hispanic 2%
Percent of Students with Transfer-in Credit: 35%
Special Adult Programs: Yes

HOW DOES IT COMPARE?

College Experience: ★★
Market Response: ★★★
Chance of Getting Out: ★★★★
Chance of Getting In: ★★★★★
Career Development Potential: ★★★★
Total Cost: Average Tuition
Shorter than Average Time to Graduation

MOST POPULAR AREAS OF STUDY

Major Clusters: Analytical/Computational, Social Sciences
Most Popular Majors: Education 30%, Business 29%, Psychology 19%

UNIQUE FEATURES

— Fall, spring, and summer flexible undergraduate course scheduling-day, evening, weeklong, including an accelerated degree completion program in leadership for working adults.

— Human scale career-oriented programs with average class size of 1:11 that enables faculty and administrators to relate to each student's educational needs and career aspirations.

Eastern Mennonite University
1200 Park Road
Harrisonburg, VA 22802
www.emu.edu, (540) 432-4000

COLLEGE PROFILE
Tuition 2002-2003: $16,000
Average Freshman Institutional Aid Award: $4,108
Percent of Students who Receive Freshman Institutional Aid Award: 96%
Average Student Loan: $5,902
Undergraduate Enrollment - Fall 2001: 1,104
Average Class Size: 20
Demographics of Student Body: African-American 7%, Asian 1%, Hispanic 2%, Caucasian 85%
Percent of Students with Transfer-in Credit: 22%
Special Adult Programs: Yes

HOW DOES IT COMPARE?
College Experience: ★★
Market Response: ★★★
Chance of Getting Out: ★★★
Chance of Getting In: ★★
Career Development Potential: ★
Total Cost: High Tuition
Shorter than Average Time to Graduation

MOST POPULAR AREAS OF STUDY
Major Clusters: Analytical/Computational, Verbal
Most Popular Majors: Business 17%, Education 16%, Health Professions 12%

UNIQUE FEATURES
— EMU will help students combine stimulating courses, credit for work and life experience and a project to finish what they started: a college degree. Attend class one night a week. Study in a small group with other working adults. Major in Management & Organizational Development or Nursing. Students may complete their studies in about 15 to 16 months.

— General Education programs require 9 semester hours of cross-cultural education. Most students choose to fulfill requirement with international experience.

Hampton University

Tyler Street
Hampton, VA 23668
www.hamptonu.edu, (804) 727-5000

COLLEGE PROFILE
Tuition 2002-2003: $10,990
Average Freshman Institutional Aid Award: $7,231
Percent of Students who Receive Freshman Institutional Aid Award: 66%
Average Student Loan: $3,596
Undergraduate Enrollment - Fall 2001: 4,965
Average Class Size: 25
Demographics of Student Body: African-American 90%, Asian 1%, Caucasian 8%, Hispanic 1%
Percent of Students with Transfer-in Credit: 4%
Special Adult Programs: Yes

HOW DOES IT COMPARE?
College Experience: ★★★
Market Response: ★★★★
Chance of Getting Out: ★★★
Chance of Getting In: ★★
Career Development Potential: ★★★★
Total Cost: Average Tuition
Average Time to Graduation

MOST POPULAR AREAS OF STUDY
Major Clusters: Analytical/Computational, Quantitative
Most Popular Majors: Biology 12%, Psychology 11%
Business Management 10%

UNIQUE FEATURES
— Hampton is the first Historically Black college or university to offer the Ph.D. in nursing.

— Each year, Hampton faculty members are cited for outstanding achievement in a range of scholarly activities, including teaching, research, writing, and the arts. Some 67 percent hold doctoral or other terminal degrees in their respective fields—and all share a commitment to excellence in education.

Longwood University
201 High Street
Farmville, VA 23909
www.lwc.edu, (804) 395-2000

COLLEGE PROFILE
Tuition 2002-2003: $4,661
Average Freshman Institutional Aid Award: $2,459
Percent of Students who Receive Freshman Institutional Aid Award: 19%
Average Student Loan: $3,026
Undergraduate Enrollment - Fall 2001: 3,552
Average Class Size: 25
Demographics of Student Body: African-American 10%, Asian 2%, Caucasian 86%, Hispanic 2%
Percent of Students with Transfer-in Credit: 20%
Special Adult Programs: Yes

HOW DOES IT COMPARE?
College Experience: ★★
Market Response: ★★★
Chance of Getting Out: ★★★★
Chance of Getting In: ★★★
Career Development Potential: ★★
Total Cost: Low Tuition
                    Average Time to Graduation

MOST POPULAR AREAS OF STUDY
Major Clusters: Social Sciences, Analytical/Computational
Most Popular Majors: Education 22%, Business Management 20%, Social Sciences 14%

UNIQUE FEATURES
— As part of its master plan to bring technology into the classroom and prepare graduates for the rapidly changing technological workforce, Longwood University has entered into a partnership with Dell Computers to provide affordable laptop computers to students.

— Small classes (avg.=25) and a favorable faculty/student ratio (1:14), provide an opportunity for both professors and students to develop close, personal relationships

Norfolk State University

700 Park Avenue
Norfolk, VA 23504
www.nsu.edu, (757) 823-8600

COLLEGE PROFILE
Tuition 2002-2003: $3,120
Average Freshman Institutional Aid Award: $4,212
Percent of Students who Receive Freshman Institutional Aid Award: 20%
Average Student Loan: $2,999
Undergraduate Enrollment - Fall 2001: 5,890
Average Class Size: 20
Demographics of Student Body: African-American 90%, Asian 1%,
    Caucasian 6%, Hispanic 1%
Percent of Students with Transfer-in Credit: 4%
Special Adult Programs: Yes

HOW DOES IT COMPARE?
College Experience: ★★★★
Market Response: ★
Chance of Getting Out: ★★
Chance of Getting In: ★★★★★
Career Development Potential: ★★★
Total Cost: Low Tuition
                   Longer than Average Time to Graduation

MOST POPULAR AREAS OF STUDY
Major Clusters: Verbal, Analytical/Computational
Most Popular Majors: Interdisciplinary Studies 21%,
                       Business Management 14%, Social Sciences 11%

UNIQUE FEATURES
Today, the University is proud to be one of the largest predominantly black institutions in the nation. Furthermore, it is committed to pursuing its vital role of serving the people of the Hampton Roads area.

Old Dominion University
5215 Hampton Blvd.
Norfolk, VA 23529
www.odu.edu, (757) 683-3115

COLLEGE PROFILE
Tuition 2002-2003: $4,262
Average Freshman Institutional Aid Award: $3,565
Percent of Students who Receive Freshman Institutional Aid Award: 24%
Average Student Loan: $3,565
Undergraduate Enrollment - Fall 2001: 13,098
Average Class Size: 28
Demographics of Student Body: African-American 23%, Asian 6%,
   Caucasian 67%, Hispanic 3%, Native American 1%
Percent of Students with Transfer-in Credit: 56%
Special Adult Programs: Yes

HOW DOES IT COMPARE?
College Experience: ★★★
Market Response: ★★★★
Chance of Getting Out: ★★★
Chance of Getting In: ★★★★★
Career Development Potential: ★★★
Total Cost: Low Tuition
Longer than Average Time to Graduation

MOST POPULAR AREAS OF STUDY
Major Clusters: Quantitative, Analytical/Computational
Most Popular Majors: Health Professions 23%, Business Management 17%, Social Sciences 10%

UNIQUE FEATURES
— Teletechnet: A pioneer in distance education, Old Dominion developed the nation's largest televised distance learning network and a Career Advantage Program.

— Old Dominion is the only four-year doctoral institution in America to guarantee every undergraduate a work or internship experience that is faculty-directed and degree-related.

— Maglev: Through a partnership with private industry and government, Old Dominion is the site of the Maglev Transportation System's demonstration track, which will be the first magnetically levitated passenger-bearing train in the nation.

City University
11900 NE 1st Street
Bellevue, WA 98005
www.cityu.edu, (425) 637-1010

COLLEGE PROFILE
Tuition 2002-2003: $7,280
Average Freshman Institutional Aid Award: $1,730
Percent of Students who Receive Freshman Institutional Aid Award: 1%
Average Student Loan: $6,970
Undergraduate Enrollment - Fall 2001: 3,573
Average Class Size: 25-30
Demographics of Student Body: African-American 4%, Asian 7%, Caucasian 58%, Hispanic 2%, Native American 1%
Percent of Students with Transfer-in Credit: 75%
Special Adult Programs: Yes

HOW DOES IT COMPARE?
College Experience: ★★
Market Response: ★★★
Chance of Getting Out: ★★
Chance of Getting In: ★★★★
Career Development Potential: ★★★
Total Cost: Low Tuition
               Average Time to Graduation

MOST POPULAR AREAS OF STUDY
Major Clusters: Analytical/Computational, Applied Quantitative
Most Popular Majors: Business Management 54%, Computer Information Sciences 28%, Liberal Arts 7%

UNIQUE FEATURES
— With City University's variety of hours and programs, students can always fit their studies in with their lifestyle.

— Evening and weekend classes are ideal for working adults. Community and technical college transfer students can study full- or part-time in City's day programs.

— If classroom instruction is inconvenient, students may choose the Distance Education option.

Eastern Washington University
526 5th Street
Cheney, WA 99004
www.ewu.edu, (509) 359-6200

COLLEGE PROFILE
Tuition 2002-2003: $2,964
Average Freshman Institutional Aid Award: $2,540
Percent of Students who Receive Freshman Institutional Aid Award: 63%
Average Student Loan: $3,036
Undergraduate Enrollment - Fall 2001: 7,567
Average Class Size: 20
Demographics of Student Body: African-American 3%, Asian 3%, Caucasian 76%, Hispanic 4%, Native American 2%
Percent of Students with Transfer-in Credit: 49%
Special Adult Programs: n/a

HOW DOES IT COMPARE?
College Experience: ★
Market Response: ★★★★
Chance of Getting Out: ★★★★
Chance of Getting In: ★★★★★
Career Development Potential: ★★
Total Cost: Low Tuition
Longer than Average Time to Graduation

MOST POPULAR AREAS OF STUDY
Major Clusters: Analytical/Computational, Social Sciences
Most Popular Majors: Education 21%, Business Management 20%, Social Sciences 8%

UNIQUE FEATURES
Through internships, students receive academic credit by working for employers in positions related to their major field of study and career interest. An internship enables students to explore their career interests if they haven't yet decided on a major, and sample their career choices now to test out and confirm or reshape their career goals.

Saint Martin's College
5300 Pacific Avenue SE
Lacey, WA 98503
www.stmartin.edu, (360) 491-4700

COLLEGE PROFILE
Tuition 2002-2003: $16,600
Average Freshman Institutional Aid Award: $6,100
Percent of Students who Receive Freshman Institutional Aid Award: 86%
Average Student Loan: $4,241
Undergraduate Enrollment - Fall 2001: 1,100
Average Class Size: 20
Demographics of Student Body: African-American 9%, Asian 6%, Caucasian 70%, Hispanic 5%
Percent of Students with Transfer-in Credit: n/a
Special Adult Programs: n/a

HOW DOES IT COMPARE?
College Experience: ★★★
Market Response: ★
Chance of Getting Out: ★★★
Chance of Getting In: ★★
Career Development Potential: ★★★
Total Cost: High Tuition
                    Average Time to Graduation

MOST POPULAR AREAS OF STUDY
Major Clusters: Analytical/Computational, Social Sciences
Most Popular Majors: Business Management 33%, Psychology 15%, Social Sciences 10%

UNIQUE FEATURES
Saint Martin's offers a student-faculty ratio of 13:1 and outstanding education in 22 undergraduate majors and six graduate programs. Saint Martin's is notable for its strong, caring community and for its excellent value. Tuition is among the lowest for private colleges and universities in Washington state.

University of Charleston
2300 MacCorkle Avenue SE
Charleston, WV 25304
www.uchaswv.edu, (304) 357-4800

COLLEGE PROFILE
Tuition 2002-2003: $16,500
Average Freshman Institutional Aid Award: $4,522
Percent of Students who Receive Freshman Institutional Aid Award: 67%
Average Student Loan: $4,500
Undergraduate Enrollment - Fall 2001: 1,092
Average Class Size: 20
Demographics of Student Body: African-American 3%, Asian 1%,
    Caucasian 80%, Hispanic 1%
Percent of Students with Transfer-in Credit: 46%
Special Adult Programs: n/a

HOW DOES IT COMPARE?
College Experience: ★★★
Market Response: ★
Chance of Getting Out: ★
Chance of Getting In: ★★★★
Career Development Potential: ★★★
Total Cost: High Tuition
                  Average Time to Graduation

MOST POPULAR AREAS OF STUDY
Major Clusters: Quantitative, Analytical/Computational
Most Popular Majors: Health Professions 24%, Business Management 12%,
                        Education 9%

UNIQUE FEATURES
— "Experience UC Day" is a University Open House and Scholarship Competition which is held on two Saturdays during the Spring. Prospective students are invited to attend one of these days after they have been accepted to the University of Charleston. "Experience UC Day" is the ONLY time students can compete for over $340,000.00 in scholarships.

— UC offers outcome-based curriculum, experiential credit, and frozen tuition.

Alverno College

3401 S. 39th Street, Box 343922
Milwaukee, WI 53234
www.alverno.edu, (414) 382-6000

COLLEGE PROFILE
Tuition 2002-2003: $12,000
Average Freshman Institutional Aid Award: $2,058
Percent of Students who Receive Freshman Institutional Aid Award: 76%
Average Student Loan: $3,759
Undergraduate Enrollment - Fall 2001: 1,808
Average Class Size: 20
Demographics of Student Body: African-American 26%, Asian 2%, Caucasian 61%, Hispanic 8%, Native American 1%
Percent of Students with Transfer-in Credit: 1%
Special Adult Programs: n/a

HOW DOES IT COMPARE?
College Experience: ★★★
Market Response: ★★★★★
Chance of Getting Out: ★★★★
Chance of Getting In: ★★
Career Development Potential: ★★★★
Total Cost: Average Tuition
Shorter than Average Time to Graduation

MOST POPULAR AREAS OF STUDY
Major Clusters: Analytical/Computational, Quantitative
Most Popular Majors: Business Management 29%, Health Professions 17%, Communications 13%

UNIQUE FEATURES
Alverno was one of six colleges in the country rewarded with a "genius" grant by the John D. and Catherine T. MacArthur Foundation for its innovative approach to liberal arts education.

Cardinal Stritch University
6801 N. Yates Road
Milwaukee, WI 53217
www.stritch.edu, (414) 410-4000

COLLEGE PROFILE
Tuition 2002-2003: $12,480
Average Freshman Institutional Aid Award: $7,115
Percent of Students who Receive Freshman Institutional Aid Award: 61%
Average Student Loan: $3,324
Undergraduate Enrollment - Fall 2001: 3,123
Average Class Size: 18
Demographics of Student Body: African-American 16%, Asian 2%, Caucasian 72%, Hispanic 3%, Native American 1%
Percent of Students with Transfer-in Credit: 5%
Special Adult Programs: Yes

HOW DOES IT COMPARE?
College Experience: ★★★★
Market Response: ★★
Chance of Getting Out: ★★★
Chance of Getting In: ★★★
Career Development Potential: ★★★★
Total Cost: Average Tuition
Average Time to Graduation

MOST POPULAR AREAS OF STUDY
Major Clusters: Analytical/Computational, Social Sciences
Most Popular Majors: Business Management 70%, Health Sciences 30%

UNIQUE FEATURES
Cardinal Stritch University has helped adults enhance their careers for more than 60 years. Founded in 1937, Cardinal Stritch University was the originator of business degree programs designed for busy, working adults. Classes meet only one night a week with a weekly study group.

Wisconsin Lutheran College
8800 W. Bluemond Road
Milwaukee, WI 53226
www.wlc.edu, (414) 443-8800

COLLEGE PROFILE
Tuition 2002-2003: $14,970
Average Freshman Institutional Aid Award: $6,730
Percent of Students who Receive Freshman Institutional Aid Award: 100%
Average Student Loan: $2,668
Undergraduate Enrollment - Fall 2001: 634
Average Class Size: 20
Demographics of Student Body: African-American 1%, Asian 1%, Caucasian 94%, Hispanic 1%
Percent of Students with Transfer-in Credit: 7%
Special Adult Programs: n/a

HOW DOES IT COMPARE?
College Experience: ★★★
Market Response: ★★★★
Chance of Getting Out: ★★
Chance of Getting In: ★★
Career Development Potential: ★★★
Total Cost: High Tuition
Average Time to Graduation

MOST POPULAR AREAS OF STUDY
Major Clusters: Analytical/Computational, Verbal
Most Popular Majors: Communications 22%, Visual and Performing Arts 13%, Education 12%

UNIQUE FEATURES
Each course throughout the curriculum is designed to help students develop the skills they will need in any career: critical thinking, communicating, and decision-making. Students will learn to write well, verbalize their ideas, develop productive work habits, and work as a team member.